THE
FRUIT OF THE
SPIRIT

Cultivating Christian Character

STUART BRISCOE

Harold Shaw Publishers
Wheaton, Illinois

ISBN 0-87788-366-1

Cover design by David LaPlaca

Library of Congress Cataloging-in-Publication Data

Briscoe, D. Stuart
    The fruit of the Spirit : cultivating Christian character / D. Stuart Briscoe.
        p.   cm.
    ISBN 0-87788-366-1
    1. Fruit of the Spirit.   2. Christian life—1960-   I. Title.
BV4501.2.B729   1993
234'.13—dc20   92-42055
                                                     CIP

99   98   97   96   95   94   93

10   9   8   7   6   5   4   3   2   1

Contents

1 Spirit Life 1

2 Love 13

3 Joy 29

4 Peace 45

5 Patience 63

6 Kindness 81

7 Goodness 95

8 Faithfulness 107

9 Meekness 123

10 Self-Control 139

11 No Orchids for
   Wisconsin 157

1
Spirit Life

I guess you could say there were two kinds of people in my home town: those I liked and those I didn't! Alf Doidge was my favorite. He was funny, friendly, played cricket, and taught me to do crossword puzzles. But I didn't like my headmaster, Frank Sandon, who looked like Josef Stalin and, in my estimation, had problems making the punishment fit the crime. Everybody liked Jack Woodruff. He made coffins by day and sang tenor by night. Even his laugh was melodious, and his high notes were a thing of wonder. So, too, were his bulging veins as he reached the grand climax of his arias and recitatives. I don't think I liked Norman Nicholson. He had long hair, wore sandals, went for long walks, and wrote poetry. We suspected he looked down his long nose at us and didn't like what he saw!

Now that I am a lot older and a little wiser, I realize my likes and dislikes were reactions to the way people behaved. Now I make an effort to understand the *why* of others' behavior. One of my friends was behaving quite erratically until the doctor discovered a blood sugar imbalance, gave her medication, and dramatically changed her behavior. The "why" was blood sugar of all things! My easygoing son, Pete, picked up two technical fouls in a basketball game, to his chagrin and my dismay. On inquiry I discovered he'd picked up this uncharacteristic behavior from watching the pros! The "why" was his desire to emulate those he thought were "cool." Guerrilla fighters go to suicidal lengths to make their point and engage in acts of phenomenal courage (or stupidity, depending on the eye of the beholder). The "why" is their passionate belief in the validity of their cause.

Passionate belief does not necessarily lead to belligerent behavior. Mahatma Gandhi's benign passivity was expressive of fiercely held convictions. So, too, was Luther's unyielding stance at the Diet of Worms and Cranmer's unflinching fortitude in the flames of execution. C.T. Studd's belief that no sacrifice which he could make was too great when compared to the sacrifice of Christ on his behalf led him to a life of unmeasurable dedication and hardship. In China, India, and Africa C.T. Studd relentlessly pursued his calling, even when his body had become what he described as a museum of tropical diseases.

Belief and Behavior

James explored this link between behavior and belief in his epistle, under the headings of "faith" and "works." He insisted that faith without works is dead, reminding us not only that belief behaves, but that correct belief behaves properly. The Lord Jesus made a similar point when he explained that people could be known by their fruits in much the same way that trees and plants can be identified by their produce. With telling wit he noted that grapes don't grow on thorns, and figs don't do well on thistles! In other words, the caliber of belief can be measured to some extent by the quality of behavior.

The extraordinary beliefs of Christians can reasonably be expected to produce dramatic behavior patterns. For instance, like Studd, those who believe in the sacrificial death of Christ are more likely to adopt a sacrificial life-style than those without similar convictions. Those who understand the release of forgiveness in Christ know something of the motivation to forgive those who trespass against them. People who believe in a wise Creator have a sense of purpose and direction in life not available to those who believe otherwise, and the person who is convinced of the holiness of God has a clearly developed sensitivity to righteousness and morality quite different from the person whose standards have no such solid and unchanging base.

The uniqueness of Christian belief and experience is found in the person of Jesus Christ. Unlike other religious pioneers and founders, Jesus is portrayed as being himself the satisfactory sacrifice for the sins of the world. Moreover, he is presented as having risen from the dead and subsequently living in the power of an endless life. This powerful life is no abstract theological concept but an all-powerful dynamic released in the believer through the indwelling presence of the Holy Spirit. It is one thing to believe that Christ died for the sins of the world—no doubt this belief affects behavior. But it is entirely different to believe that Christ died for me and then rose again to live within me through the Holy Spirit. To believe this is to be introduced to vast possibilities of unique behavior.

Paul united the idea of fruit with the indwelling life of Christ through the Spirit in his expression "the fruit of the spirit," and he left no room for doubt about what he meant when he described the fruit in great detail: "But the fruit of the Spirit is love, joy, peace, patience, kindness, goodness, faithfulness, gentleness and self-control . . ." (Gal. 5:22-23).

Just for fun I once asked two secretaries, "How many fruits of the Spirit are there?" One said, "Eight," and the other replied, "Nine, I think."

We opened a Bible and counted, and the one who had guessed nine said, "I wasn't sure!" The other one said, "I was certain there were eight." I replied, "You're both wrong."

They gave each other the kind of knowing look that women share when dealing with obdurate men and said, "Of course we're not both wrong. There are nine."

"Why then," I asked, "does it say 'the fruit of the Spirit is' rather than 'the fruits of the Spirit are'?"

This may have seemed like hairsplitting, but I think the expression "fruit of the Spirit is" is significant.

On the rare occasions I go grocery shopping with my wife, I usually gravitate toward the produce section. I love the variety of colors and shapes and smells, but I always have to fight a terrible urge to pick the bottom apple in the painstakingly built pyramid. I watch customers pick up the plums and squeeze them. They lift grapes up to the light, polish apples, inspect oranges, and suspiciously look at the bottom of the little green baskets of strawberries. Then they make their choices.

It is not uncommon for Christians to treat the fruit of the Spirit in the same way. Some people are very loving and squeeze love for all they can get out of it. Others are joyful to a fault and spend much time polishing their jokes and shining their teeth. Faithful people take everything seriously and carefully hold their motives up to the light, and the self-controlled peer under the baskets of their actions, looking carefully for any sign of overripeness. But like buyers in a fruit store, they sometimes concentrate on the fruit that interests

4

them or comes easily to them, without bothering with other aspects of the fruit of the Spirit. Sometimes the very loving are not self-controlled, and not infrequently the joyful are not at all gentle with those they razz. It's hard for gentle people to be faithful when faithfulness requires drastic action, while occasionally the faithful have been known to exercise their faithfulness with such enthusiasm that their kindness has been open to question.

If we think of *fruit* rather than *fruits*, we take away the freedom to be picky about the fruit we like and the behavior we choose. We lock ourselves into a position of recognizing that all aspects of the fruit, whether or not they come easily, are to be desired and cultivated. We will also recognize, realistically, that under some circumstances one aspect of the fruit may be more appropriate than another, without in any way suggesting that one is more important than another.

The fruit of the Spirit is to be seen not as a collection of unrelated fruits that can be selected or neglected according to personal preference, but rather as a composite description of all-around behavior that is the direct result of a relationship with the living Lord who indwells his people by his Spirit.

A friend of mine, when he was a young boy, used to get out of his bedroom after being banished there for bad behavior. His means of escape was an old fruit tree situated outside the bedroom window. One day his father announced that he planned to cut down the tree, as it had not borne fruit for years. That evening the boy and his brothers purchased a basket of apples and under cover of darkness climbed into the tree and tied fruit on the unproductive branches. The next morning they waited anxiously to hear their father's response. On seeing the remarkable phenomenon, the man shouted to his wife, "Mary, I can't believe my eyes. The old fruit tree that has been barren for years is covered with apples. It's a miracle, because it's a pear tree!" My friend added, "But Dad understood more than he admitted; the tree was not chopped down."

Fruit of the Spirit, Character of God

The connection between fruit and root is obvious not only in matters of horticulture, but also in spiritual things. The aspects of the fruit of the Spirit listed by Paul could just as easily be listed as characteristics of the nature of God. The love of God is probably his most universally appreciated characteristic. His joy in creation and his special rejoicing over his children is clearly taught. That he is Jehovah Shalom, "the God of Peace," is fundamental to our spiritual well-being, and without his patience there would be no such thing as opportunity for repentance. Believers bask in the fact that his severity is tempered by his goodness and find their assurance in his unchanging faithfulness. In fact it is important to remember that Jehovah, in his self-revelation to Moses, used many aspects of the fruit of the Spirit to describe himself.

And he passed in front of Moses, proclaiming, "The LORD, the LORD, the compassionate and gracious God, slow to anger, abounding in love and faithfulness, maintaining love to thousands, and forgiving wickedness, rebellion and sin. Yet he does not leave the guilty unpunished; he punishes the children and their children for the sin of the fathers to the third and fourth generation."
Exodus 34:6-7

Christian behavior prompted by the Spirit is similar to divine behavior, and Christian character bears marked similarities to the character of God. The connection of root and fruit is clear to the eye of faith.

The Fruit of the Spirit	The Character of God
Love	God is love (1 John 4:16)
Joy	He will rejoice over you (Zeph. 3:17)
Peace	The God of peace (Heb. 13:20)
Patience	He is patient with you (2 Pet. 3:9)
Kindness	His kindness to us (Eph. 2:7)
Goodness	I will see the goodness of the Lord (Ps. 27:13)
Faithfulness	Great is your faithfulness (Lam. 3:23)
Meekness	I am gentle and humble (Matt. 11:29)
Self-control	He has shown strength [related Greek word] (Luke 1:51, RSV)

But there is a problem relating Christian behavior to the character of God: It's so easy to be overwhelmed by the immensity and holiness of God's character!

I'm reminded of the story of the little boy who was disappointed with the smallness of the egg his chicken laid. So he went downtown, returned with a large parcel and, kneeling down in front of the bantam, unwrapped the parcel, revealing an ostrich egg. Holding it before his unsuspecting fowl, he said, "Take a good look at this and try harder." In a sense there is as much chance of Christians emulating the divine example and reproducing the divine character as there is of chickens laying ostrich eggs. Yet it must be admitted that the link between the fruit of the Spirit and the character of God clearly exists in Scripture.

It must also be understood that Christians are commanded to reproduce this unusual quality of life. The command may not be, "Take a good look at this and try harder," but it is there nevertheless. To many people the idea of commanding fruit to grow seems ludicrous. I have even heard preachers deriding such an idea. They have great fun imitating someone telling a tree to grow and twisting themselves into knots as a means of showing how impossible it is for branches to obey commands through their own efforts. The Scriptures, however, do not seem to regard the idea as ludicrous, as will be clearly seen from the following quotations:

The Fruit of the Spirit	The Command of Scripture
Love	Love the Lord; Love your neighbor (Matt. 22:37-39)
Joy	Rejoice in the Lord (Phil. 4:4)
Peace	Seek peace and pursue it (1 Pet. 3:11)
Patience	Be patient with everyone (1 Thess. 5:14)
Kindness	Clothe yourself with kindness (Col. 3:12)
Goodness	Let us do good to all people (Gal. 6:10)
Faithfulness	Be faithful, even to the point of death (Rev. 2:10)
Meekness	Show true humility toward all men (Titus 3:2)
Self-control	Add to your knowledge self-control (2 Pet. 1:5-6)

Our Efforts and God's Work

The problem of feeling overwhelmed with the number of areas in which we are to pattern ourselves after God's character seems to disappear when we remember that when a metaphor is used to aid communication, it does not mean that every aspect of the metaphor necessarily applies to the illustration. If I call my six-foot-five-inch son "a big horse" when he slam dunks, that does not mean he eats hay and whinnies, although feeding him hay might be cheaper! And my daughter who "runs like a deer" does not have four legs, pricked-up ears, and a little white tail.

The fruit of the Spirit is most definitely the result of inner workings of the blessed Holy Spirit, without which no such thing as Spirit life would be possible. But that does not mean that the life is produced without human involvement and obedience. The blending of the supernatural working of the Spirit and the normal activities of humanity are facts of spiritual truth and experience that can never be fully understood and will therefore always be the subject of debate. No one, after 2000 years of debate, has fully and satisfactorily explained the unique blending of the divine and the human in the Incarnation. The perennial debate on where the human effort ends and divine work begins in the mystery of biblical inspiration shows no sign of abating and probably never will. To ignore human obedience and stress divine intervention in the spiritual life not only requires a selectively indifferent approach to Scripture, but also overlooks the wonder of the divine-human relationship that is the essence of knowing God.

I have a theory that our approach to Scripture is more conditioned by our personalities than we may imagine. There are some people who by nature are "laid back." They say things such as I once said to a German friend when he was getting impatient with me: "Gunter, it won't matter in a hundred years—so relax." To which he replied, "I know it won't matter in a hundred years, but it matters now." The laid back hang loose—they "take it easy" and exhort others to "cool it" with the encouraging thought that it is "no sweat."

The opposite type is organized and detail conscious. These people love seminars and sharp pencils, and they establish goals with intermediate goals that are attainable and measurable. They have checklists (and ulcers?) and wear intense expressions and "suitable clothing."

These two types don't always appreciate each other. The hang-loose accuse the organized of organizing the Holy Spirit out of business. To which the organized respond with suggestions that perhaps things would not need so much organizing if the laid-back would turn up on time, do what they promised, and get their act together!

The main point of these differences, for our purposes, lies in the tendencies for the laid-back to love the analogy of fruit because it allows them to be as inactive as a branch resting in a trunk and for the organized to latch on to the commands with the same kind of intensity and responsibility that they attack everything else. While one group, with knowing smiles, reminds us, "The battle is the Lord's, you know," the other group, with clenched teeth, roll up their sleeves and "fight the good fight with all their might."

The truth is not found in either emphasis, nor is it in some never-never middle ground, but in *both*. Spirit life is the product of both Spirit activity and human response. It comes from obedience to God's commands to love, be patient, kind, and self-controlled, but it also takes dependence on God's power, through the Spirit, to make it possible.

I was once required to don cumbersome breathing equipment and march bravely into a ship's bulkhead that was full of black, oily smoke and bright orange flames. The only reason I even went close to the situation was because I was commanded so to do! But I went in totally dependent on a colleague who was busy pumping oxygen along the lifelines. Obedience to the command without dependence on the supply would have left me a cinder. Dependence on the supply without obedience to the command would have left the bulkhead a cinder. Both were necessary if the job of extinguishing was to be done.

In much the same way, Christian experience requires the balance of both. I have found it helpful, when bearing this in mind, to neglect the aspect of truth that comes easily and concentrate on the one that may require some degree of discipline. For instance, when I find myself in a situation where it is easier for me to relax when I ought to be taking action, I concentrate on plain obedience, knowing the trusting part will come along. On the other hand, when I confront a situation to which I instinctively react with drive and determination, I consciously try to remember to depend on the resources that are mine through the Spirit. The balance has been known to produce in me godly behavior that would otherwise not have been in evidence. It is the difference between human living and Spirit life.

QUESTIONS

1. What is the relationship between belief and behavior? Give some examples of their results in individuals' lives.

2. How significant is the expression "the *fruit* of the Spirit"? Why?

3. Describe the relationship between the fruit of the Spirit and God's character. How can the Christian cause the fruit to grow in his own life?

4. Where do you think your effort ends and God's will begins? What is the role of the Holy Spirit in this growth?

2
Love

My wife, Jill, is the most gentle, loving, supportive wife a man could ever wish for, and I love her. My golden retriever, Prince, is the most idle, disobedient, unreliable, sneaky animal known to man, and I love him, too. It's true, I love both my wife and my dog, even though they are so utterly different!

Of course, while I use the same word, *love*, to describe my feelings and attitudes toward them, obviously I don't hold them in identical esteem. My critics might add that they know I don't feel the same about my wife and my dog, because when it rains I send my wife out to get the dog! But don't believe them!

Enjoying the English language as I do, I have to admit that it is definitely impoverished in some areas. Perhaps the peculiar need of the British to hide their emotions, to maintain the traditional British stiff upper lip, has made the English language deficient in the area of feelings. The sad fact of the matter is that we have to use *love* for wives and dogs and steaks and golf, because there aren't too many other words from which to choose!

When we hear words, we put them through the filter of our preconceptions. The word love is no exception. If I say, "I

13

love my wife," my hearers hear, "I love my wife the way a man loves his wife." When I say, "I love my dog," the hearer never thinks, "Aha, here we have a weird man who loves a dog as he loves his wife," but rather, "He loves his dog the way a person loves a dog." So our understanding of love is largely related to our hearing filter, and accordingly ideas about love are widely divergent.

"Love is a warm puppy," I read one day on an ornamented plaque. "Love is never having to say you're sorry," I heard from a movie. "Love is a sickness, full of woes," I learned in high school from the Bard of Avon. "Love is like the measles, everybody catches it sometime," I was advised by a cynical friend. And to my astonishment I learned one day, "Love makes the world go round."

Moreover, I discovered love is something you "make" on occasions and "fall into" at other times. It has been known to produce broken hearts and goose bumps, loss of appetite and starry eyes, and has inspired some to die and others to kill. Love may make the world go round, but it certainly causes a lot of confusion in the process!

This confusion has found its way into spiritual experience because of the high priority given to love in biblical revelation. "God is love," we are told. "Love the Lord your God," we are instructed. "Love your neighbor as yourself," and even, "Love your enemies." In case we are tempted to regard loving as an option, our Lord defined it as a "new commandment" and went so far as to insist that by it others would recognize us as his disciples. Moreover, we note that love heads the list of the fruit of the Spirit (Gal. 5:22-23) and is called the greatest in the short list of things that will abide (1 Cor. 13:13).

When we bring the confusing array of ideas about love to bear on the numerous statements and instructions related to

Spirit life, we produce a bewildering difference of spiritual experience and expectation. Love in the spiritual sense, for some, is little more than a warm glow or a good feeling. For others it is an insipid acceptance of anything and everything, a tolerance of the intolerable, or even an embracing of the forbidden, because it makes them happy.

Three Kinds of Love

What then is this love of which Christians speak so often and sing so loudly? Naturally we must turn to the Scriptures for answers. The Scriptures were not originally written in English and therefore do not suffer from the limitations of the English language. In the Greek language the words *eros*, *phileo*, and *agape* were available to those who wished to speak of love. Each word had its own special emphasis and accordingly was capable of presenting differing shades of meaning.

Eros

For instance *eros*, which is not found in the New Testament, is the word from which we get our English word "erotic." It has to do with the sexual aspects of love that the Scriptures clearly teach are good and proper when experienced in the context of marriage according to the biblical pattern. It is unfortunate that biblical Christians have not always been at their biblical best when dealing with sex or *eros*. As a result we have tended to surrender the high ground of God's gift of sex to the hordes of those who would debate it and abuse it. This reticence is surprising when we recall that the Scriptures speak of human sexuality and sexual behavior with the warmest commendation both for our delight and survival. Of course, they also speak openly and bluntly about all manner of sexual deviance and aberration. *Eros* is not dirty because it came from the clean hands and pure heart of a holy God. Sexuality is not to be spoken of with a snicker, because it was among those things loudly and clearly pronounced good by God at creation.

But *eros*, for all its goodness, is not the love of which we speak; for good as it is, it is limited. *Eros* desires to possess the desirable, for self-satisfaction and personal benefit. This egotistical type of love must be exercised only in the context of a broader understanding of love demonstrated and enjoyed in the commitment of marriage, or it will inevitably degenerate into a self-seeking and self-serving caricature.

Phileo

Phileo, from which we get such words as "Philadelphia" and "philanthropy," is companionship and friendship love. It is not egotistic, like *eros*, but has connotations of mutuality. The boy-meets-girl event portrays it admirably.

"I like you," says he shyly.

"I like you, too," she responds.

Encouraged, he adds, "I like you more than I said."

"Me, too," she murmurs, blushing.

"I love you," he blurts.

"What?" she asks breathlessly.

"Nothing," he mutters.

"Go on, say it," she urges.

"Okay, but don't laugh. I love you."

"I love you, too."

Bells ring, fireworks explode, violins play, and they get married and live happily ever after for six weeks. But then the relationship takes an ugly turn.

Appearing from behind the paper at breakfast, he says, "I've had it with burned toast."

She responds, "Just be thankful you're not in Ethiopia, with the starving millions."

"When I see the food you prepare, I sometimes wish I was."

"Well if life is so bad for you, why don't you just go?"

"I think I will."

All too often this kind of thing happens in modern relationships, although the disintegration takes a little longer in most cases! The problem is that *phileo* love, like *eros*, is limited. While the boy's statements of love continue on the up and up, so do hers, but once his affections start on the downward path, hers come tumbling after. Herein lies much of the problem of many modern marriages. It isn't that they lack love. More often they are built on limited love—*eros* and *phileo*. *Eros* is sensual, but the senses are fickle. *Eros* is physical, but the body has a habit of growing in the wrong places. *Phileo* is great until it hits the skids, but once it does, it takes a great force to stop its momentum.

Agape

Agape is the word for love that makes all the difference in the New Testament. It describes God's love for us and the love that God looks for from us. *Agape* is the fruit of the Spirit. *Agape* is the stuff of which the New Commandment is made, and it is *agape* that is to be directed toward God, neighbor, and enemy. *Agape* is altruistic, in sharp contrast to *eros* and *phileo*. It is not related to sensual considerations or physical attractiveness. It does not depend on harmonious atmosphere, winsome coaxing, or tender wooing. *Agape* is the fruit of a decision that commits itself to the well-being of the beloved, regardless of the condition or reaction of the one loved. When *eros* comes under the umbrella of *agape*, sexual abuse and infidelity are out of the question, because both would fail to foster the well-being of the loved one. When *agape* throws a shield over *phileo*, the commitment to the other's well-being is more powerful than the urge to reaction. *Eros* unguarded by *agape* is open to all manner of sexual "freedom," which is actually bondage to selfishness and slavery to personal satisfaction. But *agape* protects *eros* in the bond of marriage and provides deep satisfaction without abusing the other person. When *phileo* wants to walk out in a rage and slam the door because of the other's insensitivity, *agape* says, "Hold it a moment, perhaps by slamming the door you would further injure a hurting person and thereby show no concern for his well-being. Why not swallow hard, stick around, and do something kind and helpful, or maybe just keep quiet!"

The powerful desire for personal satisfaction can dominate a life so thoroughly that any means is justifiable to meet such an end. The right to react as we wish and to get even, if necessary, is so deeply ingrained in the modern mind that it has become a perfectly acceptable mode of behavior. But neither of these positions is acceptable in *agape* country. When we talk about Spirit life, we talk about denial of some commonly accepted "rights" and the surrender of many normal contemporary reactions. *Agape* is a challenge to end all challenges, and that may be why it is so little understood and even less taken seriously.

This is particularly sad in light of the fact that Christianity is based on red-blooded *agape*. The model for *agape* love is the character of God demonstrated in his dealings with mankind. "God is love" is surely one of the most profoundly simple statements of literature. God's love for mankind was first shown in creation, more sharply focused in the long and trying relationship between Jehovah and the children of Israel, and brought to excruciating clarity in Christ. The love of God went to the trouble of creating us, providing for us, and instituting the means of preserving us. God's love rested on Abraham, blessed Isaac, wrestled with Jacob, rebuked through prophets, governed through kings, ministered through priests, waited through rebellions, persisted through captivities, and showed itself in many and varied forms through Israel's long and checkered history.

But bright as the revelation of love had been, it shone with a new, surpassing brilliance when Christ was born. It was the Father's *agape* that overlooked personal enjoyment of Christ's beautiful presence in glory and for the sake of earth suffered the pain of his departure for faraway places. *Agape* persisted when the earthlings treated the loving presence of the heavenly infant at best with callous indifference, symbolized in manger and stable, and at worst with murderous plot. Misrepresentation and character assassination from threatened religious leaders were accepted with the equanimity of *agape*. *Agape* went to the homeless and the defenseless, the oppressed and the despised; reached down to emaciated beggars; took common clay and worked healing to the blind; wept with the mourners; and with compassionate understanding, rejoiced with those who found even the smallest events of life important enough to cause joy. Finally *agape* arrived at a cross and with strong meekness accepted humiliation and hostility, shame and scoffing, sin's dread load, and the searing heat of pent-up divine passion on behalf of those who gambled at the cross's foot and cursed from the cross's side.

Agape looked in understanding at a widowed mother's grief and spoke a forgiving, loud proclamation of Paradise to a repentant hopeless one.

Jehovah's love for Israel was infinitely more than *eros* and *phileo*, or it would have tired and retired long years before Christ. The Savior's love for a lost world was far greater than *eros* and *phileo*, or it would have returned posthaste to heaven at the first sign of rejection. But *agape*, with untold patience, bore with Israel and stayed with rejection for the sake of the loved lost ones. Their condition was appalling, their reaction to love was worse. There was nothing about them that deserved such love and could make any rightful claim to such patience and sacrifice. It was *agape* that flowed relentlessly from heaven and in full force swept into its current people, who became known as Christ's disciples and reflectors of his love. It is this kind of love, far removed from thoughts of warm puppies and moonlit roses, which is to be the goal of the Christian and the mark of the disciple.

Love Is a Choice

I suspect that even when we understand the uniqueness of love in the life of both Christ and the Christian, our built-in concepts and popular ideas still have a powerful influence on our attitudes toward loving. For instance, love, for both Christians and unbelievers, is more often related to "liking somebody a lot" than choosing to be concerned.

The leader of one of our small groups told me one day that the group had decided to disband. Apparently it was the only thing they had agreed upon for some time! When I asked the reason for the decision, I was told that they had been together so long they had learned how much they disliked each other. Their problem was not uncommon.

Normally when we attend worship we put on special attitudes and perform in ways that are found acceptable. This is in marked contrast to our behavior immediately prior to entering the sanctuary. When each in a family of five wants the bathroom at the same time on Sunday morning, tempers get frayed. Mother's frustrations are not aided by the fact that breakfast is getting cold and father is sitting in the car, honking the horn. The drive to the church, with mother finishing her hairdo and son finishing his toast while daughter does her nails, is not helped by an argument over the radio. Mother wants Christian music, the kids want "something more lively and less like a funeral," and Dad wants the sports. On arriving at the church parking lot, the last space is taken by someone who cuts in, driving a car that says on the rear bumper, GOD LOVES YOU, AND SO DO I. By this time everybody is fit to be tied. But a remarkable thing happens on entering the foyer. Smiles appear, gracious words are spoken, deep interest in the well-being of others is shown, and thoroughly delightful Christian courtesy pervades the atmosphere. What happened? The family stopped behaving "naturally" and started performing church behavior actions!

The small group I mentioned had been "putting on" church behavior for many weeks, but the strain had begun to tell. One by one the relationships became threadbare, nerves became frazzled, and people started to find out what others were really like, and they didn't like what they saw. "We have no alternative but to disband," said the leader of the group.

"There is an alternative," I suggested. "Now that you know what you are really like, in the same way our families know what we are really like, you could decide to do what Christians are called to do, and that is to choose to love those you dislike." This was a startling thought to the leader, and later the group greeted it with some degree of skepticism until we looked at the Scriptures together and saw the meaning of *agape* as modeled in Christ and mandated to Christians. The group did not disband, but engaged in some healthy confrontations and commitments and continues to this day.

God, Self, Neighbor, and Enemy

Love, we are told, is to be directed toward God, self, neighbor, and enemy. To love God requires the activity of heart, soul, and strength. It is not so much a matter of liking him, anymore than it has to do with sexually desiring him, feeling romantic about him, or getting goose bumps when thinking about him. Rather, to love God means that we care for him, his well-being, the furthering of his plans, and the accomplishment of his purposes. Our hearts enable us to understand him, while our souls are responsive to what we know; and with our strength, we put muscle and sinew to work, practically, to show our appreciation for him and our readiness to do what he desires.

From this perspective of loving him we can properly love ourselves. This idea of self-love raises not a few Christians' eyebrows, because we know that Christians are taught to deny themselves. I think the problem is that we have confused selfhood with selfishness. There is no way we can endorse the inordinate self-love of our contemporary world or encourage the total abandonment of self-improvement and self-gratification, which appear to be the stuff of which modern society is made. But that does not mean that in our understanding and love for God we should fail to appreciate our selfhood, which is the product of his creative genius, or our uniqueness, which is part of his eternal plan. We must appreciate the worth that accrues to our beings because of his love, which made us children of the living God. In fact, if we love God and are committed to him and his purposes, we have no alternative to being concerned for our own well-being as the persons he made, redeemed, gifted, and called.

This correct view of self in turn leads to a proper love of neighbor. When I see myself in the perspective of God's work in my life, I begin to realize that the despicable person who is my neighbor—whose radio blares at night, whose dog wanders on my lawn, whose cars get parked on my grass, and whose kids smoke dope on my street—is actually a person of derived worth and who accordingly warrants caring about. My love for God helps me to see myself, which in turn helps me to see my neighbor, which, of course, in turn—in theory at least—helps me to understand the call to care for the well-being of my enemy. For when all is said and done, the line between neighbor and enemy is very finely drawn at times, and the difference may be more academic than real! Love to God, self, neighbor, and enemy are bound together in the Spirit life.

The Practical Effects of Love

But we must beware of becoming too theoretical about love, because if love is anything, it is practical. There is no more beautiful statement of love in action than Paul's ode to love recorded in his Epistle to the Corinthians. "Love" he wrote to the people of Corinth, the city notorious for its perverted view of love,

Is patient, love is kind. It does not envy, it does not boast, it is not proud. It is not rude, it is not self-seeking, it is not easily angered, it keeps no record of wrongs. Love does not delight in evil but rejoices with the truth. It always

protects, always trusts, always hopes, always perseveres.
1 Corinthians 13:4-7

It is no coincidence that many of the descriptive phrases of this passage mirror very closely the composite picture of the fruit of the Spirit, and this has led some Bible students to assume that love is the fruit of the Spirit and all the other descriptive words are used to convey love in its varied activities.

This may or may not be the case, but I do know for a fact that studying the description of love was one of the most powerful influences on my life. If, as Paul says, love "is not rude" then my overpowering approach to some people was totally unacceptable. To realize that "love is not self-seeking" was deeply convicting in the light of my own self-assertive approach to leadership. Reading that "love is not easily angered" spoke volumes about my short exasperation fuse, and then to be reminded that "love keeps no record of wrongs" meant a deep reevaluation of relationships where purportedly everything had been forgiven and forgotten, but in actuality partially submerged resentments still lurked.

To take Paul's words to the Corinthians off the velvet shelves of literature and place them on the hard edges of unacceptable behavior was to be humbled, chastened, and challenged. I had little difficulty being impatient with church members who, instead of realizing what a superb sermon they had just heard, seemed incapable of asking anything but the most inane, irrelevant questions! The love in evidence in such circumstances was more love for my oratory than for the people's nurture.

But it was primarily in the area of family and marriage that the deficiencies of genuine love became apparent. Was my concern really for my children or for my plans for my children?

Were the pressures they labored under the product of their perceptions of my expectations or genuine, healthy pressures necessary for wholesome growth and maturity? Was I subconsciously pushing them to the limit to be something that deep down I had wanted, yet not had the opportunity to be? What was my goal—my gain or their good? The answers to those questions held the reality of my love, and I needed to know the truth, however painful.

My wife, whom I have loved for many years, could reasonably have expected more consideration from me. She had never suggested it and in no way had hinted that my attitudes had ever caused her pain. But I began to realize the depth of my own self-involvement and the degree to which she had been expected to go along with it.

I began to see that being concerned for Jill's well-being was a noble phrase full of resounding emptiness until filled with actions large or small that spoke clearly of interest and sensitivity. Letting her know I would be late, expressing appreciation for a job well done, taking a load, volunteering an involvement, speaking honestly about what I really felt, and looking her in the eye when she needed a little attention became evidences to her of my love. I even came to the point of accepting the fact that she would never balance a checkbook if she lives to be one hundred. Therefore, the expectation should be shelved for eternity; if heaven could remedy the problem, fine, and if not, even that would not be allowed to destroy my eternal bliss. Loving her meant not expecting her energy level to equal mine. It included recognizing her freedom to be a little down once in a while and even surprising her with a flower, a meal, or a ball game, just as a treat.

None of these things "just happened." Without exception they came as the result of a deepening understanding of love and a conscious decision to do it!

When projected from the confines of church and home into the cold reaches of a self-absorbed world, the need for love became even more apparent. The hurting homes, the fractured relationships, the constant stream of evidence of man's inhumanity to woman and vice versa were so loud in their cries for loving concern and practical, sensitive involvement that they could not be ignored if any claims to discipleship love were still being made. The lost condition of large segments of the population both on the doorstep and in the deserts and jungles—concrete and otherwise—could not be disregarded in the name of *agape*, and increasingly steps to be part of the answer had to be taken.

Agape moved heaven to earth in mighty force, and *agape* lifts earth to heaven in transforming power. *Agape* sent God to people and ever since has raised people to God. No wonder it is the greatest experience of Spirit life.

QUESTIONS

1. Why is there so much confusion concerning the meaning of the word *love*? How did the Greek language avoid this?

2. Define *eros*, *phileo*, and *agape*. How are they different from each other? How can *agape* affect *eros* and *phileo?*

3. Give some examples of how God modeled his love for us. Use the Bible stories mentioned in this chapter.

4. Consider the relationship between love for God, love for self, and love for one's neighbor. How are these bound together in the Spirit life?

5. What can you do to respond to the challenge of meeting a hurting world with God's love?

3
Joy

Anyone who has traveled in the Holy Land is aware of the special significance of the Sabbath. The Arabs celebrate it on Friday, the Jews on Saturday, and the Christians on Sunday. This means that it is possible to arrive on the West Bank on a Friday to find everything closed, move on to Jerusalem on Saturday, in time to find the Jewish quarter as quiet as a tomb, and travel on Sunday only to find the Christians have shut up shop. This is great for people who don't enjoy shopping, but not so good for the diehard bargain hunters. Of course, once the Sabbath is over, the place quickly comes to life.

Tel Aviv is the place to be on Saturday night. Once the sun has set, the crowds flood into the public places, and soon the fragrant, warm air is full of the sounds of music and dancing. The contrast between the joyous music and the quiet Sabbath is quite dramatic as well as surprising. I must admit that until I saw and heard the Jewish people in such a lighthearted mood, I had always thought of them in terms of holocausts, quick wars, dark clothes, and somber music in a minor key. I didn't know they experienced so much joy!

My approach to the Old Testament was not dissimilar. I saw it as a collection of foreboding books full of violence and vendettas and prophetic pronouncements of unrelenting doom and gloom. Imagine my delight and surprise to find a broad strand of joy running through these ancient Scriptures—a joy as welcome and unexpected as the music of Tel Aviv on Saturday nights.

The same kind of reputation exists for Christians. They give the impression of being very serious people, even to the point of dullness and gloominess. They speak much of sin and judgment, the cross and shed blood. Their hymns sometimes extol a God with a frowning countenance, known as the Ancient of Days. They exhort each other to rescue the perishing and speak often of a great Tribulation, the Beast, Armageddon, and the man of sin. Their seriousness in the light of the human condition is well founded, and their solemnity in the light of God's self-revelation is more appropriate; nevertheless their lives are supposed to be characterized by joy.

Words of Joy

Both the Hebrew of the Old Testament and the Greek of the New use a number of different words to express the joy and rejoicing that is an aspect of the fruit of the Spirit. When David returned home after defeating Goliath, he got a hero's welcome as the women met him "singing and dancing, with joyful songs and with tambourines and lutes" (1 Sam. 18:6). The Hebrew word used is *simchah*, which has connections with the thought of bright and shining. The eyes of a two-year-old at a Christmas tree or a bride walking down the aisle to meet her bridegroom shine with a brightness and sparkle that testify clearly to joy that may be inexpressible in any other way. This joy is recognized in the Old Testament.

Another word for "joy" is *masos*, which means "leaping" or "jumping." The man who was healed as he sat at the Beautiful gate of the Temple is a good example of leaping and jumping joy (Acts 3:1-10). Much to the embarrassment of Peter and John, who had been instrumental in his dramatic healing, he insisted on going to worship with them, but his joy knew no bounds (pardon the pun!). No doubt he caused quite a stir by his unconventional entrance. But this kind of joy is perfectly permissible in biblical thinking.

Rinnah is yet another word that conveys the idea of exuberant expression of joy, with particular reference to "shouting." There are some Christians who like this kind of expressive, even explosive, demonstration of joy and others who are not so sure.

As a preacher I must say that it is encouraging to hear people in the congregation let rip an occasional "amen," particularly if they get it in the right place, but an ongoing, unthinking stream of hollering can be distracting for all concerned. On one occasion when I was preaching, a dear pastor friend of mine was in the congregation. He was getting somewhat carried away with his joyful appreciation of the message, so much so that he was saying more than I was able to squeeze in. So with tremendous emphasis I said something that was quite unacceptable, and as I suspected, he let out a resounding "Amen." To which I responded by saying, "You don't agree with what I just said, do you?" "What did you just say?" he queried with a sheepish grin. "Sorry I wasn't listening; I was enjoying myself too much." This kind of extreme exuberance notwithstanding, there is room for shouting, praising, joy in God's pattern of acceptable behavior.

Then there is the word *gil*, which has its roots in "moving around in a circle." This is not meant to encourage those whose lives are spent getting nowhere, but rather to encourage the kind of joyfulness that can sometimes be shown only in slightly zany behavior. My old dog, when he has been shut inside during a long, hard winter, shows his joy at springtime by grabbing his tail in his teeth and chasing it round and round until he rolls over exhausted but exhilarated. He doesn't know it, but he has got a solid dose of *gil* joy.

So we see that Old Testament joy can be shown in the quiet shining of the eyes, the boisterous leaping and jumping of the extroverts, the noisy exclamations of deep-felt thrill, or even the fun capers that don't always bear rational inquiry but adequately demonstrate emotional delight.

That God approves of his people being joyful is thoroughly attested in Scripture. They were instructed to come before him "with joy" in the regular religious festivals, and David, who was roundly criticized by his wife for his exuberance in returning the ark, would have certainly agreed with the statement that "it is fitting for the upright to praise him" as they "sing to him a new song; play skillfully, and shout for joy" (Ps. 33:1-3). And Zephaniah gives us an interesting insight into the character of God when he writes:

The LORD your God is with you,
   he is mighty to save.
He will take great delight in you,
   he will quiet you with his love,
   he will rejoice over you with singing.
Zephaniah 3:17

There is a particularly beautiful connection between the Greek words for joy and grace. *Charis* is the word for "grace," which is at the root of all Christian experience. Were it not for the grace of God, there would, of course, be no salvation, so it is hard to imagine a more fundamental word than *charis*. It also bears the meaning of "delightful," and the connection between graceful and delightful is easy to see.

But the word for "joy" is *chara*. Perhaps we can put it this way: *charis*, when properly understood in all its delightfulness, produces a sense of *chara* in many-faceted delight. This thought should be so foundational to the believer that every thought of grace should produce an exclamation of joy.

This was certainly the case with the angels who, at the beginning of the Christian era, made their proclamation of the gospel message with "great joy." Knowing what they did of the human condition, the glories of heaven, and the mysteries of divine grace about to be revealed, they could not contain their joy, and it should never be forgotten that the original New Testament gospel statement was made in such circumstances. With this in mind, the Lord himself, the One who would make salvation possible, progressed through life with a sense of joy. It must be admitted that Jesus is more often thought of as weeping over Jerusalem, rebuking Pharisees, or grieving over bereaved families and erring humans, but through it all there was an unmistakable glow of joy and delight. On one occasion when Jesus was particularly aware of the spiritual conflict in which he was involved and the eternal consequences for all concerned, he was moved to praise as he was "full of joy through the Holy Spirit" (Luke 10:21). On numerous occasions he was seen enjoying the delights of a wedding, rejoicing in the bright eyes of children, relaxing with close friends, and, much to the consternation of his critics, sharing the company and experiences of some who were not exactly ascetic in their life-style.

Joy in the Early Church

Because of Christ's joy, it is not surprising that the church founded by his disciples should, in the midst of its intense suffering, exhibit a resilience of joy that could not be overlooked.

They met in less than favorable circumstances, but nevertheless, "ate together with glad and sincere hearts, praising God and enjoying the favor of all the people" (Acts 2:46-47). They encountered people in the most unusual situations, but were equal to the task of making the Christian gospel attractively relevant, and the results were dramatic and exciting. The secretary of the treasury for Queen Candace of Ethiopia was a case in point, and when Philip had finished with him, he "went on his way rejoicing" (Acts 8:39). Perhaps he disappeared into the desert sunset leaping, jumping, shouting, bright and shining, chasing his tail in circles! I doubt it, but the joy was evident all the same.

The joy of the early believers was related to their tremendous sense of relief and triumph after the Lord rose from the dead. For them to see Christ risen and in command after the overwhelming, crushing sense of defeat that attended the Crucifixion and their ignominious desertion worked wonders for their joy. Then they saw him ascend to glory with the promise of his triumphant return in power and dominion. This focused their attention on heaven, where the angels were already rejoicing over sinners coming to repentance and presumably were practicing for eternity, when their joy would know no bounds as the fullness of redemption began to be experienced and expressed. If angels could rejoice so much over repentance, what would they do when everybody finally arrived home for the consummation of their redemption? The thought, no doubt, stimulated much joyous anticipation.

It is against this biblical background that we need to address the tendency to fall into depression and the alarming acceptance of morose and morbid behavior in the community of joy.

Joy in God's Good World

Shortly before I was born, my parents went out on a limb and bought a small business, only to find the economy was sliding into a depression. They worked long and hard to make ends meet, and they succeeded—but only just. Life was hard, and work was the order of the day (and night). Commitment to lay leadership in the local church was also a top priority, so church work and business left little room for anything else. Then came the war, and things became even more tight and tense. But we all survived, chastened and toughened, ready to meet whatever life would send along next.

We didn't have to wait long before cancer made its ugly entrance, followed by coronaries and death. The nature of our circumstances and the particular situations the family was required to confront did not allow for much relaxation or flippancy. We just didn't have time for too many "extras."

I believe this background is why I didn't realize until much later in my life that God "richly provides us with everything for our enjoyment" (1 Tim. 6:17). Work and its significance and importance I understood. Service was a way of life I never questioned. Being weary with well-doing appeared to be the normal condition of those who lived in our house, and that was about it. Although I lived all my boyhood in England's Lake District resort area, I never climbed a single mountain. I had been blessed with an athletic body but was continually reminded that Paul said, "bodily exercise profiteth little" (1 Tim. 4:8, KJV). The theater was frowned on; art and music played no significant part in our lives; and travel just wasn't a possibility. As a result many things related to culture were unknown, and many years went by until I could begin to accept that some of the things I had no interest in or knowledge of had been put by God into his marvelous world for my enjoyment. In fact, it came as something of a shock to realize that perhaps my concept of the separated life had separated me from enrichment and unto impoverishment.

I read a book called *Run While the Sun Is Hot*, Harold Fuller's account of a trip visiting missionaries in Africa. The descriptive passages were exciting to me. Fuller had wandered around with his eyes open and enjoyed the color, the drama, the fragrance, the idiosyncrasies, the uniqueness, the humor of animal, plant, insect, and human. My blinders came off and I began to see all there was to see and enjoy all that God had made available to his children.

I went to hear a performance of Beethoven's Ninth Symphony. Evidently he had decided that all the instruments of the orchestra were inadequate to express his feelings and had taken the extraordinary step of introducing the human voice in solo, quartet, and chorus. I knew that the baritone would stand and protest in song against all the dissonance of life reflected in the music and, using Schiller's less-than-sublime poetry, would insist that everyone's thoughts should turn to joy. But I was not really prepared for the heights of joy, the sheer volume and intensity of emotion generated by the musicians as the symphony came to a conclusion. I knew that on the opening performance of the symphony in Vienna, Beethoven had sat in the front row, following the score and beating time. When the crowd rose in tribute, the only person unaware of what was going on was Beethoven himself. Twenty years earlier he had lost his hearing. The Ninth Symphony had somehow been born in the inner recesses of a man's experience—a man incapable of hearing the very expression of his own understanding of joy. What the stimulus for such joy could have been we can only surmise. That there was a stimulus of profound proportions goes without saying.

I began to explore the stimuli of God's rich world with new ears and eyes intent on being moved to joy in the glad appreciation of his provision.

The southern edge of the Sahara Desert is one of the least exciting places in the world to visit and one of the least comfortable places on earth to live. But it was there that I met a missionary from Australia. He had lived for years in that area, not surviving, but triumphing in the most spectacular way. It was my observation that he had managed to be interested in everything that was going on around him because he believed that God had put all the things there for his enjoyment. One day he started talking about the birds of the area. I was amazed when he told me how many varieties he had identified. Then he talked about rock formations. I could see only rocky sand or sandy rock, but he had seen much more. He went on to talk about tribal customs, cultural differences, water tables, modern pumping equipment, the climate, and of course, because he was Australian, cricket. On every subject there was evidence of interest and appreciation, involvement and joy at being part of God's creation. I realized that if people can be so full of joyful life in that desert, there is no excuse for anything less than joyful appreciation of God's provision in much more amenable surroundings.

Of course there has to be the ability to see the hand of God in the smallest creature and the glory of God in the most subtle touch of beauty. This stems from the enlightening work of the Spirit and, nurtured properly, blooms into the full fruit of the Spirit.

Beauty in nature and the arts, truth in the intricacies of science and research, and love in the warmth of relationships are all given to us by God to stimulate our joy as they mirror for us the invisible attributes of God. But in addition to the revelation of God in such varied life experience, Christians are specially aware of the revelation of God in Scripture. In fact only Scripture gives us the key to unlock the meaning of revelation in other areas. Unless Scripture had told us that God can be seen in these things, we would never have known. Without the clear statement that God gave so many things for our enjoyment, we could never have been sure that our joy was legitimate.

Joy Comes from Suffering

Perhaps one of the most comprehensive statements about joy found in Scripture is the one from the pen of Paul, recorded in Romans 5. Writing about salvation, the apostle permeates his exposition with joy. "And we rejoice in the hope of the glory of God. Not only so but we also rejoice in our sufferings. . . . We also rejoice in God through our Lord Jesus Christ, through whom we have now received reconciliation" (Rom. 5:2-3, 11). The joy of which Paul writes is clearly related to our knowledge and experience of God and what he has made available to the human race. The reconciliation to which he refers includes being "justified through faith," having "peace with God," and experiencing "grace in which we now stand."

This is not the place to get into any lengthy study of these terms, but it is critical that we understand that joy comes from rightly understanding and appreciating theological truth. To be justified, to be at peace, to stand in grace is to know the exhilaration of forgiveness, acceptance, sufficiency, and assurance. To wake up in the morning bearing in mind the relationship with the Lord that makes such blessing real is to embark on a day tinged with glory and to approach life with a deep sense of well-being. To nurture carefully the appreciation of such truths through disciplined worship and devotional exercise is to feed the soul with the fuel of joy. To relate to others who know such things in their lives is to be buoyed with the positive benefits of fellowship, while sharing the discovery of grace, peace, and justification with those to whom such things are a mystery is to feel the deepest satisfaction and to know the riches of exhilaration.

To "rejoice in the hope of the glory of God" is to have a handle on the future, which eludes so many. Our world has its transformationists, its survivalists, its doomsdayists, and its escapists. Some believe that however bad things become, man is bright enough and resilient enough to be able to transform even a return to the Stone Age into a glorious society. The survivalists have a less noble vision, being primarily concerned with preparing for the worst by ensuring their own comfort in some wilderness hideaway stocked with dried food, modern weapons, and as many creature comforts as they can amass. The doomsday people have given up on the whole mess and proclaim loud and clear that time has run out and the human race is finished, while the escapists think that may be true, so there's no point worrying. They say, "Let's eat, drink, and be merry, because tomorrow we fry."

But the Christian rejoices in hope of glory! This should not be used as a rationale for a life-style barely distinguishable from other responses to the future as perceived by man. There is no justification for a brand of Christian escapism that hides in prophetic studies designed to assure the redeemed that they will not have it rough. Neither does it justify an evangelical doomsdayism that harshly delivers society to the chill winds of cruel fate. It certainly does not open the door to churchly survivalism in the happy precincts of lavish retreats from both involvement and discomfort. To rejoice in the hope of glory is to live in this world, feeling its pain, binding its wounds, challenging its presuppositions, and diagnosing its ills with no thought of self-preservation or personal disassociation, but rather with a communicable and palpable sense of the ultimate victory of the Lord and the possibility of sharing in that victory over sin and death and hell.

In addition, Paul makes the bold assertion that "we also rejoice in our sufferings." This does not mean the apostle was a masochist any more than it excuses the popular belief that Christians are exempt from suffering. We have no more freedom to derive pleasure from pain than we have freedom to assume that it will never happen to us and that if by some strange accident it does, then there will be an immediate and ultimate alleviation.

Suffering is a fact of life that goes along with the territory of a fallen world. There is no such thing as a free ride for fallen people inhabiting a fallen environment that is inextricably bound up with a fallen society. There is just too much wrong with our attitudes and stresses, our foods and our pollution, our selfishness and our outright rejection of biblical standards to provide even the remotest hope that while we are down here there will be no problems. But the Christian handles the suffering in a special way—he rejoices in it!

Paul explains that this is possible because of what the Christian "knows." Specifically, he knows that "suffering produces perseverance; perseverance, character; and character, hope. And hope does not disappoint us" (Rom. 5:3-5).

This truth needs to be peeled like an onion. The suffering on the outside needs to be peeled away to reveal the quality of perseverance that cannot be learned with pressure. The mature quality of perseverance gives way to the building of character that is able to transcend childish selfishness, which comes so easily to people of the modern era. Once character is forged through the mill of pressure and adversity, this in itself produces a quality of hope or confidence based on past experience of triumph over adversity. Of course, hope can be misplaced, and confidence can come crashing down like a radio tower in a hurricane, but not if it is grounded firm and deep in the Savior's love.

The reminder of this love comes through the ministry of the Holy Spirit. In the hardest moments he whispers, "I love you"—a sentiment that we may be reasonably expected to question. "If you love me, why are you allowing this to happen?" To which he replies, "It's because I love that I am allowing it to happen. Without trials, you won't persevere. You'll be shallow and flippant, unreliable, and superficial. But working through these things, you'll build up fine qualities of mature Christian character and, in stress, begin to show your world a confidence that can be attractive and challenging. That's what I want for you, because I love you so much."

Knowing all this and being reminded of these things at the time of suffering helps us to see suffering in a new light. Rather than something to be avoided and resented, evaded and denied, the suffering allowed by a loving Father is designed to accomplish the maturing process to which the believer is committed, and therefore it is to be embraced even with joy—not because of the sensation of pain, but because of the knowledge of objective locked in the benevolent heart and mind of the loving God.

One thing remains to be said. There are those who are so resilient or so favored that they seem to sail through life like gulls in a gale, while others wallow in the waves and sink without a trace. To the former, joy comes easily and almost naturally; to the latter it is a struggle.

Let me remind you of the balancing truths with which we started our study. Those to whom certain aspects of Spirit life are difficult must remember that it is in dependence on the working of the Spirit and in direct obedience to the commands of Scripture that these things move off the pages of orderly print into the throbbing corpuscles of flowing bloodstream.

The command is clear-cut, "Rejoice in the Lord always. I will say it again: Rejoice!" (Phil. 4:4). The resources in the Spirit in terms of teaching, revealing, and sheer power are boundless, and if further motivation is necessary, remember that "the joy of the LORD is your strength" (Neh. 8:10).

QUESTIONS

1. What kind of joy is described by *simchah? masos? rinnah? gil?* Why does it take so many words to describe this part of the fruit?

2. How are the Greek words for "grace" and "joy" related to each other? Why will an appreciation of the first cause an increase in the second?

3. Why could first-century Christians have joy despite persecution? How did this affect the spreading of the gospel?

4. Give some examples of how God can use creation to stimulate joy in the believer. What is the part of the Spirit in this? Why is Scripture important in revealing the joy God has made available for the Christian?

5. How can suffering bring about joy? Why does God sometimes allow Christians to suffer?

4
Peace

The prophecy conference was going well until one of the speakers suggested that it would be a good idea if the participants, instead of using the normal greetings, should use the one popularized by the early church. He pointed out that the believers were awaiting the return of Christ so eagerly that they habitually used the word *maranatha*, an Aramaic word for "the Lord is coming," as their greeting. The idea was warmly embraced, particularly by two little old ladies, who when they met the speaker en route for breakfast the next morning, trilled in unison, "Marijuana, brother, marijuana." They were close phonetically, but not really close at all!

Peace—in Negative and Positive Terms

Western travelers in the Middle East may wonder how close the Arabs and the Israelis are to reality when they greet people with the traditional *salaam* or *shalom*. Both words mean "peace," and no doubt, the greeting has an eerie ring in the ears of those accustomed to the sound of gunfire and bombing in that troubled part of the world. But in all fairness we should point out that their ideas of peace and ours differ considerably.

We usually define peace in negative terms, such as "absence of tension" or "cessation of hostilities," but the words *shalom* and *salaam* are more positive and contain the ideas of order and well-being. This can easily be demonstrated from the story of David and Uriah the Hittite (2 Sam. 11). When the king brought the soldier home from the front, in an attempt to cover up his nefarious conduct with Uriah's wife, he feigned interest in the well-being of the men at the battle front. "How is the *shalom* of Joab?" he asked, "and the *shalom* of the soldiers and the *shalom* of the wars?" Clearly, if *shalom* meant absence of hostilities to David, he was asking the nonsensical question, "How is the absence of hostilities of the hostilities?" Actually what David wanted to know was, "Is all well with Joab, the soldiers, and the war?" Augustine of Hippo was able to capture the ideas of both East and West in his striking definition of peace as "the tranquility of order." In my opinion this definition has not been surpassed.

When peace is regarded as the absence of tension, we may feel that the way of peace is in the manipulation of circumstances so as to eliminate stress. Quite apart from being impractical, this approach is unbiblical.

Gideon is a case in point (see Judges 6). One day when he was trying to thresh wheat in a winepress—an exercise in futility, if ever there was one—he was startled to hear himself addressed as a "mighty man of valor." Anyone less likely to receive such an accolade is hard to imagine, because at that moment Gideon was in mortal fear of the Midianites and was trying to hide his harvest from them in case they came and took it. He was no mighty man! In his own eyes Gideon was closer to a mighty mouse! However, the visitor continued to talk to Gideon and managed to persuade him that he had a very important job to do, that valor was required, and that Gideon could do it because the Lord would be his strength. Gideon asked for a sign that he was hearing and understanding it all properly, and when the sign was given to his satisfaction, he promptly offered a sacrifice to Jehovah Shalom, "God of peace." Jehovah was requiring Gideon to take actions designed to produce violent reaction, yet Gideon saw him as Jehovah Shalom—not because he was heading for a peaceful experience, but because he was going into tension with the assurance that the God of order would keep things under control and therefore Gideon could enjoy the tranquility of order.

The prophet Isaiah recorded the word of the Lord in this regard:

"I am the LORD your God,
who teaches you what is best for you,
who directs you in the way you should go.
If only you had paid attention to my commands,
your peace would have been like a river,
your righteousness like the waves of the sea."
Isaiah 48:17-18

"Peace like a river," as we so often sing, enables us to know "it is well with my soul." This wellness is not a feeling that suddenly envelopes us, but rather the sense of well-being that comes from knowing everything is under control, under the Lord's capacity as the One who "teaches you what is best" and "directs you in the way you should go."

But, of course, God's teaching, directing, and commanding require a willing spirit and a glad submission to his benevolent direction. It should never be forgotten that Isaiah immediately goes on to state that there is "no peace . . . for the wicked" (verse 22). Those who reject what is best and disregard the principles of behavior that God has ordained will understandably know nothing of the sense of well-being they would have known if they had lived their lives in obedience. It's rather like getting a new car, reading the owner's manual provided by the manufacturer, and carefully going through the service procedures. When the oil is changed regularly, when the tires are kept at the correct pressure, when the moving parts are properly lubricated, there will be a sense of well-run order. But if the old oil is left to clog up the works, under-inflated tires are run for miles, and nothing is done to counter the normal wear and tear of moving parts, it will not be long until the car will not move smoothly like a river, but more like a capsized canoe in a waterfall. The tranquility of order is only for those who carefully order their lives according to the principles of the God of order—Jehovah Shalom.

When we turn to the New Testament, we find similar themes echoed in the ministry of our Lord. Jesus told his disciples quite bluntly that they would have all kinds of trouble in the world, but that "in him" they would have peace. On the one hand they were presented with the disconcerting prospect of trouble, but on the other hand Christ's calm assuring words of peace. There was no idle promise that everything would be smooth sailing, but neither were the disciples given the impression that they were about to be cast adrift in a merciless sea of overwhelming currents. Their challenge was to discover how to balance living in the world with living in Christ.

This has been the Christian dilemma ever since. To live in Christ apart and separate from the world has been the approach of monastics and fundamentalists for centuries. To live in the world without reference to living in Christ has been the tendency of many professing believers who show little if any sign of spiritual life and vitality. To identify with a society that rejects and repudiates the uniqueness of Christ and his principles is an ongoing temptation against which disciples have always had to struggle. They have found themselves exposed to society's ills, tainted by its pollution, challenged by its needs, and touched by its hopelessness, so isolation has not been a possibility, however much they may have wished for it.

But how to live in society and triumph through it has always been the problem. And the answer is to be found in readiness to observe the teachings of Christ, as opposed to the principles of a secularized world, and to draw on the resources of Christ's indwelling presence, rather than the mechanical and organizational resources provided by a society, however enlightened and concerned.

A young black pastor told me that before he accepted his pastorate, he worked for a number of years in the black community as a social worker. During that time he was able to help ease many burdens and ameliorate much suffering, but he always felt limited in what he could do. Since becoming a pastor, however, he has been free to teach the principles of Christ and to introduce the suffering people to the saving and liberating grace of Christ. The results, he told me, have been dramatically different. In fact, he said, "I've been able to see more real results in terms of changed lives in one year in the pastorate than in all my years as a social worker."

Without in any way minimizing the sterling work done by many social agencies, it must be understood that secular society works on principles quite different from divine principles and has attitudes far removed from those of believers. Through our ability to live effectively and compellingly in the secular society, we live "in Christ" yet in the world. In this balance we can find peace in the midst of trouble. There is no better illustration of this than the Lord himself. When confronted by the hunger of the multitudes, Jesus calmly lifted his eyes and heart to heaven and handled the tension with a deep, settled sense of tranquil order. Standing before Pilate and the hostile religious leaders, he, in tune with his Father, was more at peace in the turmoil than any other person in sight.

Three Applications of Peace

There are three entirely different applications of the experience of peace for the believer. First we read about "peace with God"; second, "the peace of God"; and third, "peace on earth." Using our definition of peace as the "tranquillity of order," I would suggest that "peace with God" is the experience of spiritual order; "the peace of God" is a sense of psychological order; and "peace on earth" is the experience of relational order.

Peace with God

That there is a clear sense of order in creation is plain to see. Sunrise and sunset are entirely predictable, the tides come and go on time, seasons follow each other in order. Seedtime and harvest, cold and heat, summer and winter, as promised, do not cease. The more we look into the intricacies of ecology and the complexities of biology, the more we become aware of the orderliness of God's handiwork. At the same time, we have seen enough going wrong in the ecological and biological worlds to recognize that it is tragically possible for man to interfere with the natural order and to produce all manner of unwanted and unwarranted aberrations. The same is true in terms of spiritual realities.

Once the factor of disobedience has been introduced into human behavior, a chain of events is set in motion. Disobedience promptly introduces a feeling or a sense of disorder. Those who are disobedient may never give thought to God and have no conception of what it means to obey him; nevertheless they are aware more often than not that there is something wrong. Many a man has been utterly amoral in sexual relationships and has no conscience whatsoever about the activities in which he is engaged, yet he has been strangely aware that his life has not been working out right, that things have not been going the way he wanted them to go, even though he had granted himself total freedom to work out for himself anything he wanted.

The same is true of societies that embark on schemes at odds with the divine order. All may seem orderly at first, but then the feeling of disorder begins to appear, and in time a pervading sense of disease (or dis-ease) that leads to an overriding sense of dismay takes over. This appears to me to be the case in contemporary America.

When I arrived in the United States of America for the first time, in the mid sixties, I was both exhilarated and frustrated by what I discovered. I was exhilarated by the great positive spirit that prevailed. The "can do" approach looked at every problem as an opportunity for American ingenuity and commitment to prove itself. "No problem" was the watchword. "We'll fix it in no time" was the slogan. After living in tired post-war Europe, where everybody had tried most things and knew they wouldn't work, this positive attitude was wonderfully refreshing. But it was frustrating in that the "can do" spirit smacked of self-sufficiency, and the positive approach, at times, paid scant regard to the facts of the matter. Then along came Vietnam, with its attendant frustrations and humiliations. Mighty and resourceful America was dealt a blow to its pride. Watergate followed hard on its heels, with corruption revealed at the highest levels. Then a bunch of young sheiks who had learned their lessons well at Oxford and Harvard went home and worked out how to corner the world's economy, as providence had graciously given them a corner on the world's energy.

The resultant downturn of the economy, the ongoing build-up of the Soviet nuclear and conventional armory, a succession of administrations that appeared to be impotent to do anything other than change the program from high inflation and low unemployment to low inflation and high unemployment all contributed to the feeling that all was not well. A strange sense of dismay, of foreboding began to take over. People began to look again at the nuclear buildup, to ask questions about the nature and the value of human life. They looked with concern at the breakup of the family, and at the preponderance of narcotics used by the celebrities of stage and stadium. The feeling of dismay became pervasive.

To the believer there was nothing particularly surprising about any of this. Disobedience, whether individual or corporate, leads to disorder, disease, dismay. But equally to the believer there was no problem in recommending a solution. Those who had been disobedient could learn about being forgiven through the sacrifice of Christ on their behalf. This would lead, in turn, to a process of reeducation, allowing for the possibility that disorder could give way to correct behavior and experience. Spiritual health and knowledge of peace with God could replace dismay of spirit and a foreboding sense of hopeless gloom. That is the message of peace with God.

If you have ever seen a group of raw recruits drilling, you will have noticed that there is always at least one unfortunate person who is apparently incapable of swinging his right arm forward at the same time his left foot goes forward. Everyone else in the squad has it right except him, but he has the most profound impact on the whole group. His disorderliness creates such a sense of disruption in the ranks that the complete effect is destroyed, and the drill sergeant's composure suffers a similar fate. If, however, the unsynchronized recruit can be prevailed upon either to get in step or go and peel potatoes, a new sense of togetherness is experienced by the body as a whole. The peace of order prevails.

A young man named Trevor walked into a meeting in England one night, sat and listened to everything that was said, and at the end came to me and asked if I would help him commit his life to the Savior. To the best of my recollection he had never before been in a church and had never heard any explanation of the Christian gospel. Nevertheless Trevor appeared to understand enough to be able to make a positive response to what he had learned, so we prayed together and, after making arrangements to meet later in the week, we went our separate ways.

Later that night Trevor went as usual to the local pub, ordered his regular pint, and sat in his normal seat at the bar. One of his friends evidently noticed that Trevor was more quiet than usual and asked him, "What's wrong, Trev?"

"Nothing's wrong," he replied. "In fact, come to think of it, for the first time in my life everything's right. Up till now I've lived my life holding my breath. Now I feel I can let it all out and start to breathe." Trevor could not have explained the doctrines of faith, but he knew the reality of "peace with God," the tranquility of spiritual order.

Peace of God

The stresses of life in the modern world are producing all manner of psychological and physical reactions. Tension headaches, high blood pressure, ulcers, and coronaries are taking a heavy toll on our society, and anxiety is becoming chronic for many people. This is partially due to the fact that the demands of modern living are such that more and more people wonder if they can possibly cope. Yet strange as it may seem, it is not the new stresses that seem to be most bothersome, but some of the old problems for which even modern technology does not have all the answers and that contemporary society is impotent to alleviate. When it really comes down to it, the problems that give people the most anxiety are illness and dying. Modern medicine has done a great deal to alleviate pain and to prolong life, but it has made a burden for itself that it is unable to carry. It has raised people's expectations to unrealistic levels and produced attitudes that demand, "You heal me, or I'll sue you!" There is a kind of escapism that flees at the first signs of illness into the belief, "It couldn't happen to me." And when it is apparent that it did happen, people insist, "It shall not be allowed to take its full course with me."

It is unfortunate, to say the least, that this kind of thinking has been encouraged by Christian ministers who have promised healing for everything from terminal cancer to tooth decay. The stress of facing illness is more than many of us care to handle, and the fanciful flights to various escapist destinations solve nothing.

It's the same with death. When I moved to the United States I was impressed with the number of total strangers who visited my home to wish me well. Pretty soon I noticed that they all sold insurance! One day my visitor was talking about the necessity to be prudent in the preparation for all possibilities. "If something should happen to you, Mr. Briscoe—" he started to say, but I interrupted with, "Please don't say that. It upsets me."

He was a little startled, but tried again. "But with all due respect, sir, we must be ready if something should happen to us—"

"Don't say that," I insisted.

He looked totally bewildered and said, "I don't understand what I said to upset you."

"Then I'll tell you," I replied. "It upsets me that you talk about the only certainty as if it's a possibility. Death isn't a possibility, it's a certainty. You don't say, 'if,' you say 'when' whenever death is the subject." Then I added, "By the way, when something happens to you, what will really happen?"

The man didn't answer because he had just remembered another meeting. And that's the common way of handling death. We evade the issue by talking about it obliquely. We avoid the certainty by relegating it to a realm of unlikely possibility, because it causes us anxiety.

This does not have to be the case. Jehovah Shalom, the God of peace, is the One who is committed to working all things together for good to those who love him, who are the called (see Rom. 8:28). This favorite verse of so many believers is often interpreted to suggest that God spends his time working out every little detail in life so that good will come of it, preferably immediately. This results in many exercises of mental and spiritual gymnastics that show remarkable dexterity of thought and imagination. I have even heard believers who have been able to praise God that he worked in their irresponsibility in such a way that it was apparently

55

beneficial to all concerned that they had been irresponsible and that it seemed God had been glorified in it. This cannot be a valid interpretation of Paul's words.

The key is to realize that the good of which Paul speaks is ultimate good, which resides in glory and may never be seen on earth. If it is seen, it probably would not be recognized as good. Unless we believe this, we have no way of handling the disasters that overtake the impoverished people of the Third World, the horrendous things that happen on the mission field, and the cruel circumstances that crowd in on some people, while others apparently live charmed lives. But if we have a clear sense of ultimate good in the hand of the eternal God, who has everything in control to such an extent that his people can believe when they don't see it and can even trust him for the ultimate revelation of goodness when there is no immediate trace of anything but horror and deprivation, then we can begin to understand something of the "peace of God."

Writing to the Philippians from prison, the apostle Paul made it clear that God's people, through prayer and supplication, could make their requests known with thankfulness. He promised, "And the peace of God, which transcends all understanding, will guard your hearts and minds in Christ Jesus" (Phil. 4:7).

Modern research has clearly shown that we go through various stages and reactions in the way we handle grief. Denial: "This can't be right, get me a second opinion." Bargaining: "God, get me out of this, and I'll be a missionary." Anger: "Why me, when I've lived such a good life and my kids need me? It's not fair." And sooner or later, if we handle it maturely, comes acceptance. This is not servile submission or fatalistic shoulder shrugging, but rather an intelligent appreciation of the facts as they are and a sensible response to them.

However, for the believer, the acceptance often comes more quickly than for the unbeliever, and certainly the acceptance is more securely based. To know the ultimate outworking is in the hands of the God of the universe and to understand that the outworking will be utterly good makes it possible for the most unpalatable experience to be sweetened into acceptance and the most unacceptable circumstances to be touched with the glow of glory.

As a pastor I have seen the peace of God worked strangely and surely into the ravaged features of the bereaved. On numerous occasions as I have said good-bye to the dying they have expressed only anticipation for glory, compassionate concern for their loved ones, and an insistence that I preach the Word at their funeral! Never a touch of anxiety, except perhaps for the fear of needles or the embarrassment of intimate nursing. Only a sense of psychological order—the peace of God. This is the fruit of the Spirit.

Of course, this kind of peace does not just happen. It comes, as do all the aspects of the fruit of the Spirit, from careful obedience to God's commands as we relate in dependence to God's enabling. Those who are habitual worriers, whose lives are shrouded in the gray fogs of anxiety, need to recognize the clear command, "Do not be anxious about anything," which precedes Paul's great promise of peace, and act accordingly. This does not mean that, having spent all their lives worrying, they will suddenly stop, any more than it holds out hope that they will never get depressed and fearful again. It does mean that in the degree to which people can respond positively, when the anxieties loom large, they will turn the corner and increasingly discover peace permeating mind, emotion, body, and relationships.

Peace on earth

This brings us to the third aspect of peace. "Peace on earth" or relational order. When the angels announced the gospel, they were not guilty of hyperbole in promising peace on earth. They announced the arrival of the Prince of Peace, who would bring eventual peace to bear on human relationships, but who would also make possible in interpersonal relationships a higher order of peacefulness than had been known before.

Perhaps one of the clearest illustrations of peace in relationship is found in the experience of the early church. There had long been traditional tensions between the Jews and Gentiles, partially due to the uniqueness of Jewish faith and practice and partly due to the Gentile resentment of what appeared to be a supercilious attitude on the part of the chosen people. The Jews always had a problem being popular in whatever society they chose to settle; no doubt some of their unpopularity was well earned. In other respects the Gentiles were being bigoted and thin-skinned. When it became apparent in the early days of evangelistic growth that the church would incorporate not only Jew but also Gentile, the fur began to fly. Peter, who first went to the Gentile Cornelius, did so with some trepidation because he knew that some of his brethren would be after his hide.

And Paul, in his conviction that he was called to the Gentiles, faced considerable hostility in his efforts to bring "the Gentile dogs" into fellowship with the Jews. He dealt with the matter rather fully in his letter to the Ephesians, where he explained that Christ is our peace. At first sight it might appear Paul was referring to the ministry of Christ in bringing people to peace with God, but in actuality he was talking about Christ being the means of bringing Jew and Gentile to a position of peace with each other. What Paul explained to them in effect was that in the same way that Jews had to find redemption at the foot of the cross so, too, must the Gentiles. Imagine the surprise of a Jew who, after kneeling in repentance and finding forgiveness, looked up and saw a Gentile alongside doing exactly the same thing. They were experiencing the same salvation and discovering the same Savior, being born of the same Spirit, washed in the same blood, and being baptized into the same family. The Jew's immediate reaction would be to put as much distance between himself and the Gentile as possible and take steps to see that the society of forgiven sinners be purged of all unwelcome elements.

But Paul insisted that this could not be the case any longer. For if they had both found Christ, they had no alternative but to be part of the same body, the church.

Modern-day politicians, confronted with such a problem of reconciliation, would probably have started negotiations with one side, gotten what concessions they could, taken them to the other side, gotten whatever refinements were possible, returned to the first group, bargained with the changes in position, put various pressures to bear, and eventually worked out a compromise. They would have finished up with Jews who would give a little and become Gentilized Jews and Gentiles who would give a little and become Judaized Gentiles. And those who wouldn't give an inch would have stayed where they were, only more convinced of their own positions. In other words, the politicians would have produced four parties.

But Christ came to make peace, not to produce parties. He commanded his disciples to be about the business of building his church, which Paul calls one new person made out of both Jew and Gentile. So began the immense task of bringing into the fellowship of believers those who previously detested each other.

As time went by, it became apparent that the believers were learning the practicalities of living in peace with each other. Remarkable things began to happen. As people not known for their peacefulness, they began to make peace among believers a priority. The infant churches became models of men and women living in such a way that their little corner of the world began to enjoy and model "peace on earth."

It was this understanding that led the apostles to work so hard to bring about peace in the burgeoning churches. Not that they would accept peace at any price or that they would speak peace where there was no peace. There was no suggestion of compromise or turning a blind eye to what was sin in order to preserve the peace. But there was a willingness to recognize the great weight of responsibility for the church to be the place where peace was to be found.

Paul, writing to the Romans, was wonderfully practical when he insisted, "If it is possible, as far as it depends on you, live at peace with everyone" (Rom. 12:18). Here again we see a command that requires obedience, but it is not a harsh, unreasonable, insensitive command. Perhaps aware of his own problems with difficult people in tough situations, Paul mellows his instructions with the words "if it is possible." Let's face it, you can't live in peace with someone who insists on declaring war on you. It takes two to tango and two to enjoy peace. With great sensitivity, Paul adds, "as far as it depends on you." The apostle does not lay on us the impossible burden of living in a state of peace with everyone in a hostile world. But he does lay on us the requirement to do what is necessary from our side of the problem.

This responsibility for peace requires bringing a sense of order to problems. *What is right in God's eyes?* we must ask ourselves. *What will it take for me to get right in God's eyes in this matter? What immediate steps to reconcile the situation should I take?* After all that heart searching, it takes a little lump-in-the-throat swallowing, deep-breath taking, and approaching the person concerned to see that—as far as it depends on you—the sense of order prevails in that difficult set of circumstances.

There is no easy road to peace, but then again if it were easy, why would the Spirit be necessary?

QUESTIONS

1. Describe peace in positive terms. How does this relate to Gideon's vision of God as Jehovah Shalom?

2. How does the author describe "peace with God"? "The peace of God"? "Peace on earth"? Give some examples of each.

3. What was Paul's command concerning peace? What actions will result from a believer's taking this command seriously?

5
Patience

Life cannot be lived in isolation. There are always people with whom to rub shoulders; there are always situations and events that need to be handled. Reaction is the stuff of which much behavior is made; relationships are the environment in which life is lived.

One of the most common reactions to unfavorable situations and unpleasant people (and there is no lack of either in our world) is indignation. It may be perfectly justified, partially understandable, or downright inexcusable. Usually those experiencing it call it "righteous indignation," while those on the receiving end have a wide vocabulary with which to describe what is going on. Perhaps the most common and most relevant word for indignant reaction is "anger."

When we come to the word *makrothumia*, translated "patience" or "long-suffering" in the list of the fruit of the Spirit, it is important to notice that it means, literally, "long wrath" or "slow anger." In other words, half the Greek word for patience is "anger," and the other half is "long" or "slow." Patience, in this context, is handling anger slowly. Those of us who are familiar with the Old Testament will immediately recognize the striking similarity between this expression and the way in which God described himself to Moses: "The LORD, the LORD, the compassionate and gracious God, slow to anger, abounding in love and faithfulness" (Exod. 34:6).

So once again we see that as God himself models love, joy, and peace for us he is also the example, par excellence, of patience. This cannot be emphasized too strongly because there is a feeling among some believers that anger is sin, despite the fact that God himself expresses it, our Lord demonstrated it, and Paul encouraged believers to be angry without allowing it to degenerate into sin.

The Wrath of God

To understand patience, we need to look briefly at God's anger. We cannot help noticing that anger is an integral part of the divine nature. There is a degree of reluctance in the church to talk too much about this aspect of God's nature, and this can readily be understood.

More often than not we endeavor to understand our Father in heaven in terms of our father on earth. In my case I was horrified recently to hear my daughter's objections to the way I had treated her elder brother when they were both children. She expressed, in no uncertain terms, her disapproval of what she considered to have been my overreaction to what he did and the harshness of the punishment that I had meted out. This came as a total shock to me because I had exactly the same feeling about my father's dealings with me and as a result had tried very carefully to avoid any overreaction or unfair punishment. So both my perceptions of my father's anger and my daughter's reaction to my anger showed that ·ther of us was too impressed with father-wrath! On reflec- ·rstand that both my father and I were subject to ·ressures—he in his struggles with business in the Depression and wartime, I with the responsibilities of a large church and other ministries. These pressures often made for weariness and frayed edges that no doubt unraveled sometimes at home, and the person nearest caught the effects. As a result, the wrong person got punished, and sometimes the right person got punished wrongly. I can see that now, and it makes me nervous about father-wrath.

What really bothers me is that working from that understanding of father-wrath, there is the possibility that the anger of "our Father which art in heaven" may be seen as the same kind of thing, only magnified. God's wrath may be seen as unreasonable—overreaction married to insensitivity to the real situation. I'm convinced that many people shy away from the biblical teaching concerning the wrath of God because they divorce it from his love and righteousness and imagine that it is tainted with the stain of human wrath's imbalance and unfairness. But this cannot possibly be the case.

God's wrath must always be seen in connection with God's love. This is not too difficult, because humans who are capable of loving deeply are also liable to react strongly, particularly if the object of their love is mistreated in any way.

Some years ago in a small town in England a man escaped briefly from an institution for the criminally insane. During his few hours' liberty, he captured, raped, and murdered a small girl and was then apprehended by the authorities. At the same time he arrived at the police station under escort, the father of the child arrived, too. The father was a mild-mannered man, but when he saw the person who had murdered his beloved child, he went berserk, and it took a number of lawmen to control him. There was no incompatibility between his love and his wrath; in fact, there was a clear connection between the two. Strangely, the intensity of his love was demonstrated in the intensity of his anger. Love for the beloved was shown in anger against that which had destroyed the beloved.

The love and wrath of God must be seen as a continuum of the divine emotion for humankind. The intensity of the love of God for people is clearly mirrored in the intensity of his antipathy to that which marred his creative masterpiece. And the greatest manifestation of the love of God, the cross of Christ, is itself the fiery focal point of divine wrath. You cannot look at the cross and see love without wrath or wrath without love. The cross stands tall in human history as the epitome of the relationship between both.

Neither should God's anger be seen as incompatible with his holiness and righteousness. To think otherwise is to suspect that God the Father suffers from the defects of human fathers and vents his wrath in ways that are unjust or uncalled for. There is a righteousness about God's wrath that is at once alarming and comforting, because it will always be just and fair. There is something grossly unjust about a society that can be unmoved about a person's gross treatment of his fellow human being. A society that can observe starvation, malnutrition, moral disintegration, and uncontrolled violence without batting an eyelid is sick. People who do nothing and say nothing about grave miscarriages of justice, who wastefully spend resources on trifles and invest nothing in necessities for the underprivileged, and who see no need for concern and show no tendency to indignation are not tolerant; they are fundamentally unrighteous in their lack of indignation.

So for God not to be wrathful about much of today's world would be fundamentally wrong. Without his wrath, God would not be righteous. So in the same way that his wrath and love are integrated, his righteousness and his wrath are inseparably bound together.

But having said all that about divine wrath, we must return to the basic point of our consideration, namely, that the wrath is expressed slowly. God is a God of patience. Numerous instances of divine patience can be cited from Scripture. Perhaps the best known and the most far-reaching is found in Peter's response to the scoffers, recorded in 2 Peter 3. The opponents of the infant church were joyously pointing out that the return of Christ, which the believers had so loudly predicted, had not taken place. The reason, according to the critics, was that God was presumably slow concerning his promise, and the inescapable implication of their statements was that the Lord would not return. Peter's response is somber and powerful: "The Lord is not slow in keeping his promise, as some understand slowness. He is patient with you, not wanting anyone to perish, but everyone to come to repentance" (2 Pet. 3:9).

At the coming of the day of the Lord, judgment will be swift and final, and many will perish. God must do this because of his holy, righteous nature, but he will not do it unfeelingly. There is nothing harsh or callous about the judgment of God. It is therefore easy to understand the delay, because God is holding back the full expression of his righteous indignation against sin, in order that the sinners he loves might repent and be converted. The patience of God is designed to extend the day of grace. The slowness of God's anger is a positive expression of his love for sinners and a practical means of allowing for all manner of rectification of a bad situation before it is too late. This is divine *makrothumia*—anger properly handled!

When People Get Angry

In contrast to God's way of handling anger properly, we humans have a variety of methods in everyday use. Repression is a favorite among Christians. Working on the mistaken idea that anger is always wrong, they adopt the simple procedure of refusing to admit it exists. One lady called me in my study and said, "Now, Stuart, you must listen to what I have to say, but first I want you to know I am not angry."

I replied, "I hadn't even thought of it, but presumably you had, or you wouldn't have mentioned it."

She responded with a sudden violent explosion that nearly knocked me across the room! She'd been repressing her anger and doing nobody, including herself, any good at all.

Suppression is equally popular among those who feel that any expression of anger is unspiritual. What they make of the Lord's irritation with his obdurate disciples or his dramatic closing down of the Temple supermarket, I don't know. The suppression approach to anger is refusing to express it in volatile ways and carefully pressing it down beneath the surface, as if it were not there. Suppression never walks out in a huff, slamming the door. Suppression explains itself carefully and analytically, through pale, pinched lips, then walks quietly out of the board meeting, carefully closing the door, and goes home never to return. Resentment, hurt, coldness, fury, and bitterness abound, but nothing is said, and even less is done—only an interminable silence remains to show the deep intensity of rage. The tragedy of this reaction is that it is so often regarded as spiritual, when in actuality it is anything but. Moreover, it is deeply damaging to the health and well-being of the practitioner. All kinds of illness can result. Depression can set in, and untold damage to relationships ensue. Suppression and repression are no help at all.

No doubt some of my readers are saying, "That's not me. I let it all hang out. If I'm mad, everybody knows it, and so they should. There is never any question about how I feel. I tell 'em. Speaking the truth in love I call it." They probably are as proud of their forthrightness as the suppressors are of their self-control. Expression is their forte! But they have no cause for pride in this regard.

A former colleague of mine, Joe Ballard, is a highly qualified pastor and psychologist. He was a great counselor, dearly loved by many people whose lives he touched deeply. One day he was concluding a counseling session with a young lady just as I walked past his office. Unfortunately the young lady and I had a gentle collision, for which I promptly apologized, although it was clear no damage had been done. She, however, took one step back, drew a deep breath, and then for an apparent eternity, without repeating herself, gave a full, carefully researched exposition of my failures, the faults of my ministry, the wrongdoings of the church in general and Elmbrook Church in particular, the arrogance of the British, the mistakes of Churchill, and various other related subjects!

As a pastor I am no stranger to disillusioned people, and I endeavor to listen carefully to what they have to say and respond appropriately. But my attention in this instance was distracted by my friend, Joe, who for some reason that escaped me seemed to be quite happy about what was going on. In the end, the lady ran out of breath (although not material), and I mumbled something about hoping she felt better, and away she went.

As soon as it was safe, I turned to Joe and asked what he was looking so happy about.

Joe replied, "Catharsis, Stuart, catharsis. She didn't really mean all that. She has a lot of anger that has been building up inside her for years and she needed to get it out. She'll be a lot better now."

I was glad to know she would be a lot better, but I wasn't sure how good I felt! That, of course, is the trouble with anger expressed in uncontrolled ways.

Certainly there is a need for those who repress and suppress to be helped to express, but the damage done to others in the expression must be borne in mind and of course the specific teaching on patience must not be forgotten. Joe knew this better than I did; in fact, he probably taught me more about this than anyone.

Confession is the word on which we need to concentrate. I realize that it has very specialized connotations for some people, but my meaning is that we need to be honest about how we are feeling, first of all to God and then to the people concerned. But slowly! There is no substitute for indignant persons taking the time to explain to the Lord quietly, in simple terms, how they have been aggrieved, what it is that is hurting and frustrating them, and exactly how they sense they are reacting.

Israel's king David, who had lots of opportunities for anger in his long life of conflict and setback, talked to the Lord and also recorded what he said in poetry; hence our rich heritage of Psalms. This latter part of his action is not mandatory, of course, but it may help sometimes to write out our feelings as we are talking to the Lord about them. Then, if and when the time is ripe, we should take steps to talk to the offending party about that which is causing us concern.

Timing is essential. I have become particularly irritated with people who had complaints to make to me, but insisted on making them at the conclusion of a morning service, in the midst of a crowd of people, all of whom were seeking counsel relating to the message. This was not the best time. Many people have learned the hard way that the best time to express their hurt about something their spouses have done is not the moment they poke their noses in the door, having just finished a week at the office and battled the freeway traffic for two hours.

The manner in which we express our frustration is also extremely important. For instance, when we have a complaint, we normally address the person with a succession of sentences beginning with, "You did this" and, "You didn't do that." For emphasis we frequently add a pointing, accusatory finger and immediately put the other person in the wrong and on the defensive. Both tactics usually prove to be counterproductive.

On the other hand, if after careful confession to the Lord, we courteously and carefully approach the offending party with a genuine concern for his or her well-being, as well as a desire to make our own point, there is always a real chance that person will be responsive. The best way to do it that I have discovered is to start the sentence with "I" and to sit on my accusatory finger! For instance, if I start by saying, "I need to talk to you about something that has been causing me concern. It has gone on for a little while now, but I wanted to be careful about how I addressed the situation, and I realize that my perceptions may be completely wrong," there should not be the same defensive reaction. In my experience with this kind of thing, I have found myself more responsive to those who approach me in this manner, and I have found others much less hostile toward me.

The key, of course, is to give the delay in expressing our anger an opportunity for an act of rectification to be done, which will not only air the issue and clarify the causes of reaction but will also bring the combatants into a relationship far richer than they knew before the incident.

Obviously, anger can be caused by situations as well as by people. It is not uncommon for us to be placed in a position where our own self-expression is being thwarted, and this can lead to many problems. This is even true, for instance, in the Christian ministry. Many people who have a deep desire to serve God take the step of resigning from their jobs, cutting loose from all means of visible support, and launching out into a ministry based on faith that God will provide their needs. Then they find that the work in which they are engaged is considerably less challenging than what they recently left. To their horror they discover that "full-time Christian workers" are human in the worst way, and not infrequently they become frustrated with the situation.

One young man told me recently that in his business he was "Mr. So-and-so," who had proved his worth and was recognized accordingly, but once he went into ministry, he was a "nobody" who could apparently do nothing to the satisfaction of anybody. He added, "A year after I took the big step, I was sitting in my office asking myself, 'How could I be so dumb?'" His anger at his situation was understandable and real.

Expectations from others can also be a source of deep frustrations. A friend told me recently about the anger that built up in his life as a boy. He was the second son of the family and was unfortunate enough to have a brilliant elder brother. He was constantly compared unfavorably and blamed for everything the brothers did, whether or not he was responsible. He was generally made to feel inferior. His resentment knew no bounds, and he was well into adulthood before he was able to deal adequately with the situation with his brother and his parents.

When this kind of thing happens, the very irritations them-selves cloud the issues; harmless things are perceived as dia-bolical plots, and innocuous statements are taken as insults. The result is growing estrangement and in some cases a bit-terness that can sour everything in sight. But this must not be permitted.

The biggest problem for many is that they know they are angry and don't like the way they are handling it. They know that something should be done, but they just can't bring themselves to do it. Strong motivation is necessary if we are to handle anger with *makrothumia*.

Jesus told Peter a story about this very subject. The big fisherman had been having trouble with somebody and was trying to handle it properly, but evidently his patience was running thin. He asked Jesus how many times he needed to forgive and suggested "seven times," presumably stretching it to the limit! The Lord was not particularly encouraging when he suggested seventy times seven would be more like it and then told the famous story.

There was a man who ran up some big debts with his employer, and when it became obvious that he could not pay, he asked his master for *makrothumia*, patience. Fully recog-nizing that his master would be perfectly justified in being angry at the failure to repay, the servant asked only for some patience, or slow anger. The master went far beyond the request and freely forgave him for a phenomenal amount. With great relief and gratitude, the servant left the building and promptly bumped into a colleague who owed him money. The amount owed by the second party was one six-hundred-thousandth part of the amount the first man had been for-given. When the second man asked for some *makrothumia* to give him time to pay, the one who had been forgiven got him by the throat and began to demand, with fearsome violence, that he be repaid immediately.

Jesus had made his point with customary clarity. Those who have any concept at all of God's patience have motivation enough to move in patience toward others. Perhaps when we take the time to confess to the Lord how we feel about the situations or the people who provoke our ire, we should also take the time to recollect the patience God exhibited to us before we were saved, or in the many ways we have been slow to respond to him since that day. This in itself is powerfully motivating, as Peter discovered.

It is also helpful to remember that one of love's characteristics is patience. This has been particularly challenging to me. When I have been criticized by someone in the church or in other churches where I have visited, I have been known to react in anger. But with the passing of years and the accumulating of a little knowledge of the things of God, I have learned that my anger usually stems from indignation that they do not realize how much I know and how right I am! This, when I confront it, is so ludicrous that in my quiet moments my wrath gives way to laughter. Then I am ready to see that my reaction clearly shows little interest in the *people* expressing the concern. I reacted so quickly to what they said that it was clear that I was more concerned with their impression of me than I was concerned about being a blessing to them. But remembering that love is being primarily concerned with their well-being helps me to take the time to listen and learn and react more slowly.

There is no doubt that Paul was continually moved by a great sense of the Lord's loving patience with him. He told his protégé, Timothy, that the Lord had shown him "unlimited patience as an example for those who would believe" (1 Tim. 1:16), and much of the patience exhibited by the formerly impatient, fiery, bigoted Pharisee was directly attributable to his own experience. We must never get far from the remembrance of the Lord's dealings with us if we hope to have a chance to live even close to the patience that he requires of us.

There are many areas in which the opportunity for patience presents itself, not least in the specialized world of spiritual experience. Suffering is a case in point. Living as we do in a society that believes it has the right continually to embrace pleasure and avoid pain, we have a marvelous chance to be realistic in our handling of suffering. James wrote, "Be patient, then, brothers, until the Lord's coming" (James 5:7). And added, "as an example of patience in the face of suffering, take the prophets" (James 5:10). Then for good measure he included that great man of patience, Job, making the point that those who have a sense of God's overruling in the face of deprivation are those who can afford to approach the unpleasantness of life with much less indignation and much more patience.

Pity the person whose horizons are limited to selfish considerations, whose world is no greater than his own well-being, whose vision extends no farther than the tip of his own nose! When suffering comes, he knows of no other reaction than rage at his luck running out, fearful anger that others far more deserving of fate's blunders get off scot-free. He even rails against the God whom he has chosen to rationalize into a state of irrelevance.

The unique concept of the church requires considerable patience if it is to become more than a nice idea. Paul made this clear when he wrote: "Be completely humble and gentle; be patient, bearing with one another in love. Make every effort to keep the unity of the Spirit through the bond of peace" (Eph. 4:2-3).

As we saw in the previous chapter, the believer, having come to Christ, is required to be identified with those who belong to Christ, and this requires a willingness to accept the hard and thankless task of being a peacemaker. Jews and Gentiles, with long histories of conflicting traditions and forebears who had done reprehensible things to each other, were understandably loath to get into any deep relationships with those who had long been thorns in their flesh. But Christian fellowship required it, and the building of the fellowship, along with the breaking down of the barriers, is a job for the patient.

We had an example of this kind of patient peacemaking in our church. In the early seventies some of the young people from the heady days of the youth revolution had come to Christ but had retained not a few of their radical ideas. These ideas were manifested in dress and life-style, which were both objectionable and threatening to some of our more traditional members, who expressed their displeasure quite forcibly. Someone, however, suggested a class called Generation Bridge, to be made up of people from the different groups and life-styles, age ranges and family and educational backgrounds. It was to be by invitation only, and they were to commit themselves to thirteen weeks' involvement. The participants were gratified to be invited, so we had a much greater response than if we had just left it open to those who "felt led." They arrived the first morning, looking somewhat tense, only to discover that there was no teacher; they themselves were to lead the study on the Epistle of James.

Without going into detail, the thirteen-week commitment to learn together, to listen to one another, and to take time to understand one another was the ideal matrix in which patience could have her perfect work. At the end of the period two things happened. Those who had been in the class wanted to continue, and those who were not invited were banging on the doors, wanting to be asked.

Given the will to work as we ought to in order to maintain the unity of the Spirit through the bond of peace (and this requires all kinds of patience), I am convinced the church can become the delightfully unique society she is called and required to be.

Anyone who has tried to minister in the fellowship of believers knows that people are not easily convinced or rapidly changed. Paul is greatly encouraging in this regard, in that he experienced the same frustrations, and he clearly wanted to advise Timothy in advance that such would be the case. So he wrote to him: "Preach the Word; be prepared in season and out of season; correct, rebuke and encourage—with great patience and careful instruction" (2 Tim. 4:2).

On an early visit to Texas I was fascinated by an old pastor who used a toothpick during a seminar. I had never seen such a thing before, and the fact that he never touched it with his hands added to my wonderment. The angle of the toothpick also reflected the response he was making to what was being said. On one occasion, as the speaker spoke of the delights of ministering to the Lord's people as they waited eagerly for the Word, the toothpick jutted out, and he said, "When I look at my people, they look like hooting owls sitting on tombstones." I wondered what the people thought he looked like, particularly if he punctuated his sermons with a toothpick. There didn't seem to be an awful lot of patience there, but he may, like many of his fellow ministers, have given up on being patient with God's people. Another pastor certainly had, when he said, "I left that church because they said they wanted a pastor for the sheep, but they needed a zoo keeper for the animals!"

I have found the words of 1 Thessalonians 5:14 particularly helpful: "Warn those who are idle, encourage the timid, help the weak, be patient with everyone."

Because I happen to be rather energetic, not particularly bashful, and as strong as a horse, I have no great affinity for the idle, the timid, and the weak. So naturally, I have distinguished myself with great displays of impatience to those who fit these categories. This verse, however, made me take another look at the necessity to express patience in handling such people. For instance, while I had no desire to encourage idleness, I found that many idle people were doing nothing because they were afraid to try or didn't know how. So a little patience, instead of loud condemnation of their idleness and lack of commitment, led to an attempt to assist in showing them how and in doing things with them, instead of telling them to do them.

Once when I was leading a Bible school, I decided to take the whole student body on outreach to a nearby city. The strangest thing happened. We had an epidemic of illnesses. One young man said he couldn't go because he had lost his voice. When asked what difference that made, he said, "I can't communicate."

I replied, "You communicated that you had lost your voice!" Then I think I must have had a flash of inspiration, because I added, "You haven't lost your voice, you're chicken." And when he remonstrated, I said, "And so is everyone else, including me."

To my amazement, he said with a loud voice, "You're not!" That was the day I discovered I had a gift of healing as well as the gift of discernment! After a little encouragement to realize that he was not alone in timidity, the young man was fine, and we all went off together on our trembling way.

The weak are clearly in need of much encouragement, which they seldom receive. They may be weak because they are young and immature or because they have never had the opportunity to build up their muscles. Perhaps they are weak because they are the victims of something completely beyond their control. In whatever case, they don't need a touch of someone's temper so much as a sense of someone's patience. Major Ian Thomas, who taught me so much about working with young people and who showed unending patience with many young men over the years, had a striking philosophy. He used to tell me, "Boys will be boys. But just be patient, and boys will be men."

There is boundless opportunity for the fruit of the Spirit to blossom in patience, because our world abounds in frustrations. To see that patience grows, we need to be aware of the pressure points that stimulate reactions, be alert to the possible anger that is being generated, be conversant with the way we are handling it, and be clear in our own minds whether we want to show the fruit of Spirit life in the situation or to the person concerned. If there is a genuine desire to respond to what the Word of God says in this regard, there is no better word for us than, "Clothe yourselves with compassion, kindness, humility, gentleness and patience. Bear with each other and forgive whatever grievances you may have against one another. Forgive as the Lord forgave you" (Col. 3:12-13).

QUESTIONS

1. Describe the relationship between God's love and his wrath. How does God express his patience? His anger? Compare *makrothumia* and parental anger. What are their effects?

2. Humans often express their anger in inappropriate fashions. Name three ways this may be done. What is God's solution to this problem?

3. What three admonitions did Paul give concerning patience? How can *makrothumia* benefit churches, families, and the world at large?

6
Kindness

At one stage of adolescence I had a passion for collecting autographs. Armed with my maroon leather book, I descended on all, asking them to write something on one of the pretty pastel pages. Some of the people seemed so pleased to be asked that they took the book away with them and painted what appeared to me to be artistic masterpieces. Others were not as enthusiastic. My math teacher, who was never impressed by my procrastinating tendencies, simply wrote, "Do it now." But one little lady, in painstaking handwriting, wrote a piece of less-than-memorable poetry that I nevertheless remembered:

Life is mostly froth and bubble.
Two things stand like stone—
Kindness in another's trouble,
Courage in our own.
Adam Lindsay Gordon

I never forgot the idea that "kindness in another's trouble" has an abiding quality.

Kindness is not looked upon kindly by everyone. There are those who feel that kindness carries a cost they are not prepared to pay. It is too time-consuming, too demanding, too likely to interfere with cherished plans for privacy and self-indulgence.

For many people kindness has no place in a dog-eat-dog world. Who ever tried to handle a snarling Doberman with kindness? This was certainly Lady Macbeth's complaint concerning her husband, whom she feared was "too full o' the milk of human kindness." In the pursuit of her self-centered goals, there was no room for anything as inconvenient as taking time to be kind to those whom she felt would be much more useful out of the way. To Lady MacBeth, people existed to be used until their usefulness was exhausted, and then they were expendable. Kindness that might look at them as persons and see them as creatures of significance, whose hurts were painful and whose aspirations were real, was not a factor to be built into her relationships. When her husband was showing signs of "human kindness," which might treat people adequately, that was too much for her. Unfortunately that lady has an impressive following today!

Spirit life, however, insists that kindness is not an inconvenience to be avoided, but a characteristic to be embraced. It is not an attitude only the particularly sensitive can adopt, but rather an approach to people that is fundamentally right and proper. The Hebrew word for kindness means literally, "to bow the head, treat courteously and appropriately." If this definition is taken seriously, it is easy to see that unkindness is inappropriate and that lack of kindness is out of order. Far from being an unwelcome inconvenience, kindness is seen as a basic necessity if we wish to live with any semblance of decency and respectability.

Kindness in the Character of God

It is particularly interesting to note the role kindness plays in the Old Testament understanding of God's character. One of the basic truths of God's dealings with his people, Israel, has to do with the covenant he made with them to be their God as they were to be his people. This covenant made clear that, of all the nations of the world, the people of Israel had a special and unique place in the plan of God. He had set his love upon them and, through their father, Abraham, had promised untold blessing to them and worldwide blessing through them. The long history of these people shows clearly that they had by no means been what they were required to be, but nevertheless the covenant of Jehovah had stood firm, and he had continued to shower blessing upon them. The word used to describe this is *hesed*, sometimes translated "kindness," "loving-kindness," "love and mercy."

Theologians have long debated whether God was kind to Israel because he had made a covenant with them or whether he made the covenant because it is his nature to be kind. If this seems something like the chicken and egg debate, with particular reference to which came first, perhaps we should treat it in the same way and acknowledge that there are hens and eggs and covenants and kindness, and we are grateful for all four! That God graciously made a covenant goes without saying, and that he wants his *hesed* to be recognized is clear from the statement we have mentioned in previous chapters concerning God's self-revelation: "The LORD, the LORD . . . abounding in love *[hesed]* . . . maintaining love *[hesed]* to thousands" (Exod. 34:6-7).

When we move into the New Testament, there is a much more detailed expression of divine kindness *(chrestotes)*. For instance God shows kindness to unrepentant people to such an extent that, even when they begin to abuse his kindness, he nevertheless persists in it because of his desire to use kindness as a means of drawing them to repentance. The popular idea of bringing people to repentance is to hit them over the head with their sinfulness and dangle them over the pit to reinforce the issue. Without in any way detracting from the clear necessity to expose sin and to warn people to flee from the wrath to come, it is noteworthy that God uses kindness to break stubborn hearts.

At one stage of our parental pilgrimage Jill and I were dealing with a child who had been showing some signs of teenage discontent that could have blossomed into teenage rebellion. Late one evening my wife was surprised to receive a call from the child in question, who was baby-sitting for a friend. Jill's immediate mother response to the call was, "Is everything all right? What's wrong?"

The child said, "Mom, I wanted to call and say I am sorry for being such a little snot."

"That's great, honey, but what made you call now?" Jill answered.

"I've just been sitting here thinking about you, Mom, and it's your kindness that got to me. The worse I became, the more kind you became." There was a great homecoming that night after the baby-sitting duties were complete!

Paul speaks of the kindness of God in another form when he refers to the Gentiles as a wild olive branch grated into the cultivated olive branch of Israel, to enable them to become part of God's working in the world. God's action in doing this is the direct result of his kindness and should not be seen in any other light, according to the apostle. In other words, the kindness of God not only leads to repentance, but it gives marvelous opportunity to those who have shown little evidence that they deserve such consideration.

But, of course, the prime example of God's kindness toward us is seen in his gift of the Lord Jesus. The apostle Paul describes the full measure of God's "kindness to us in Christ Jesus" (Eph. 2:7). This kindness will not be fully understood until the redeemed in all their glory are revealed to the watching and wondering created multitudes. There is a sense in which we, as individuals down here in the midst of earth's pain and suffering, can get a feel for God's kindness. But the totality of it will only be appreciated when it is demonstrated on a cosmic scale to those angelic forces beyond our comprehension. The depth of the divine kindness will be recognized fully only when the beauty of the perfected is seen in total contrast to the imperfection with which we had become so familiar on earth that we were incapable of recognizing perfection if we had seen it. God's kindness will be evident in his interest in a tiny planet's rebellious population, despite the immensity of the cosmic whole he had created. Kindness, too, will be appreciated when the greatness of the cleansing of our sinfulness is recognized. In the purity and majesty of glory, we for the first time will understand holiness and, accordingly, will really fathom sinfulness and resultant forgiveness.

In the meantime, before we get to glory where we can fully understand the depth of divine kindness, we are exhorted in Scripture to use what we do understand as an example for our own behavior. The apostle Paul put it succinctly: "Be kind and compassionate to one another, forgiving each other, just as in Christ God forgave you" (Eph. 4:32).

Kindness Among God's People

Fortunately we not only have the sublime examples of God's kindness in Christ to motivate and perhaps even discourage us, but we also have examples of people like ourselves who did some kind things, too.

When Joseph found himself in prison through no fault of his own, he set about doing the best he could in a bad situation and ended up running the prison. While he was doing this, Joseph also found time to help out some of his inmate colleagues, particularly in the interpretation of their dreams. The cupbearer of Pharaoh was one of his clients, and Joseph was undoubtedly a great help to him, free of charge. The only thing he asked was a little kindness when the cupbearer returned to life outside the prison walls. He was returning to a position of influence, where Joseph felt he could pull some strings to get him out, and the cupbearer promised to do what he could. But as might be expected, once he did get his release, he "did not remember Joseph; he forgot him" (Gen. 40:23).

The stark contrast between Joseph's sympathy with the cupbearer's plight and the cupbearer's total lack of sympathy for Joseph's situation graphically portrays kindness and the lack of it. Kindness feels for the other person, hurts with his hurts, and takes some of the burden. Unkindness is self-absorbed and carries nothing heavier than self's petty load.

Lot, the errant relative of Abraham, who had dug a deep hole for himself in Sodom, was rescued in the nick of time before the city was destroyed. He was understandably grateful but didn't feel that he was in good enough condition to keep up with his rescuers, who seemed bent on making their escape to the mountains. He thanked them for their kindness and asked for and was granted a break, and he arrived singed and sorry in Zoar. The kindness of which he spoke was, of course, his rescuers' willingness to be expendable. The generous laying down of themselves on behalf of the helpless one was in itself a superb picture of what kindness is all about.

Perhaps one of the most delightful human interest stories in Scripture is the one concerning David and Mephibosheth. After David had survived the murderous antics of King Saul, with some help from the heir to the throne, Jonathan, he finally arrived on his very comfortable throne. Seated there one day, David asked whether there were any survivors of Saul's family, and he was informed there was a lame young man called Mephibosheth, who had been injured when his nurse dropped him as a baby. David promptly sent for the unfortunate cripple and committed himself to showing him "God's kindness." This was more than a noble thought, because he made arrangements for Mephibosheth to eat at his table and to enjoy the provisions of palace living. This kindness, we must not forget, was exhibited to the sole survivor of David's former tormentor, Saul. But, of course, it was kindness related to God's kindness to David and also Jonathan's remarkable affection for the exiled shepherd boy. David's kindness was the offspring of the kindness of others.

Three Attitudes of Kindness

From these three examples, kindness is seen in terms of sympathy, benevolence, and generosity. All are essentially practical; none is less than costly.

Sympathy

When we come to a practical application of these thoughts to our own situation, it is helpful to think first of all in terms of kind attitudes that will beget kind actions. This means developing and cultivating feelings of sympathy, like Joseph.

When confronted with someone to whom kindness may be shown, I have found it helpful to try to remember how I felt in a similar situation. It always amazes me how quickly we forget. For instance, in dealings with young people I find a tendency in myself to ignore the feelings of youth because it is so long since I was young! I look at their struggles through the eyes of experience and promptly consign their great concerns to the scrap heap of triviality.

"Why should a young man like you worry about a girl who didn't show up for a date?" I once asked one of my sons in his teenage years. "There are plenty more fish in the sea," I added with a flourish.

But he was not impressed, pointing out that he wasn't interested in fishing at the present time, and therefore the numbers of fish were not particularly relevant.

"Didn't you ever find yourself let down by someone you cared about?" he wondered.

Digging deep into the mists of memory, I did recollect something particularly hurtful that had happened so long ago it had not only healed but had not even left a scar. But I had to admit that it did hurt at the time. The lesson reminded me that sympathy, which is part of kindness, is nurtured by taking the trouble to recognize how the other person is feeling.

Sometimes sympathy is achieved by recollection, but other times it takes imagination. A lady recently asked me how I would feel if my partner of thirty-two years suddenly walked out of my marriage, for that was her situation.

I answered, "I have no conception of what that means. My wife is so utterly faithful and our mutual commitment so firm in the Lord that the thought is not even thinkable. But I can try to imagine what it must be like."

In trying to imagine, I found myself concentrating on her sorrow and sensing her grief, feeling her loss and touching ever so slightly her desolation. That is sympathy, the stuff of kindness.

Benevolence

Benevolence is a choice. Shortly after I arrived in the United States, I was invited to speak at a banquet in one of the big Chicago hotels. My wife and I decided to drive down to the Windy City together and left ourselves plenty of time to find our way around. As we approached Chicago I noticed we were getting low on gas, but I knew there would be plenty of filling stations. When we suddenly came to a halt in the fast lane of the freeway, in the rush hour, with the rain pouring down, I realized my assumptions about filling stations were as wrong as my tank was empty. I climbed out of my car, to be greeted by a chorus of horns expressing displeasure and expletives filling in the details. There was nothing I could do and less that anyone else was ready to do, so I stood in the rain, and like the sailors on Paul's sinking ship, I "wished for the day."

One particularly dilapidated car drew alongside; the driver rolled down his window. I braced myself for more verbal abuse but was relieved that his English was so bad I couldn't understand it. About fifteen minutes later the same car returned in the mass of traffic and pulled up in front of mine. The driver jumped out and without a word proceeded to fill my tank from a can. He had seen my plight, gone to a filling station off the freeway, borrowed a can, gotten back on the freeway, fought the traffic, and come to my rescue. When I tried to thank him, he shrugged and said, "You look kinda new around here. Me, I just come from Puerto Rico, Friday. Ain't nobody do nothing for nobody in this city," and with that he was gone. That was generosity, kindness in a rusty Chevy.

Generosity

If benevolence is a choice, generosity takes a chance. There's always the chance that those to whom generosity is extended will take the chance to milk the one doing the extending. This well-known factor makes many people decide not to be generous. But it demonstrates an immature attitude because not all those who are helped are ungrateful, and even the ungrateful still need helping. In my experience, the willingness to be exploited is a necessary part of all kind actions, but steps can be taken to avoid unnecessary unpleasantness.

At the beginning of our married life, Jill and I decided we would operate on the principle that we would serve the Lord. This worked itself out in the early days of our marriage through work with young people among whom no one else was active for God. We opened our home to these youths and found that they were excited to be asked into our lives. They knew, of course, "an Englishman's home is his castle," and they had enough common sense to realize that by inviting them to share our home, we showed we were in earnest when we told them we cared about them. In fact, one of them spoke for the group when he said, "They ask us into their house. Even yoboes like us!" But because they were "yoboes" (the British word for what Americans call "bums"), they were not always house-trained in the broadest sense of the word! They went everywhere they had a mind to go. No corner of our small domain was off limits in their eyes, and this led to some awkward situations, not least when our little boy woke up to find an odd-looking stranger peering at him in the dark. But this was the price that had to be paid, the chance that had to be taken.

However, there came a point when enough was enough, so we simply put an eye-level sign on the staircase, which read, AND WHERE D'YOU THINK YOU'RE GOING? That got the message across, and the difficulty was more or less resolved. Most issues with that group rarely got past the "more or less" state of resolution. But one thing became very clear, and that was the blossoming of many of those youngsters under the warmth of generosity they felt and enjoyed. They more than repaid our kindness in the years to come.

Once the decision to engage in the cultivation of kind attitudes has been made, it is not too difficult to find avenues for kind action. Starting right at home, there is abundant opportunity for spouses to try a little kindness. For my own part this has meant a willingness to try listening with a sympathetic ear to the troubles my wife is having with things that cause me no trouble at all. This is not because she is easily troubled so much as I am remarkably insensitive to some troublesome items in life.

Jill insists that my favorite expression is, "I don't anticipate any major difficulty," and she threatens to put it on my tombstone. (My response is to wonder what makes her think I'm going first. I feel fine and don't anticipate any major problems!) In my opinion this is a great attitude to have, particularly since I have it. But I do admit that it isn't always appropriate. For instance, when it is quite clear that my optimism is misplaced, that disaster looms, and that when I board the plane with a cheery smile and lighthearted wave, my wife will be left with that which I did not anticipate but in which she will undoubtedly participate, there is a problem. My attitude isn't good enough, and a little sympathy and a lot of kind involvement is clearly called for!

Generosity has a special place in Christian experience. But it should not be limited to the offering plate. We do have a terrible tendency to be miserly with expressions of appreciation. Some of us give the impression that saying a heartfelt thank you hurts too much and sitting down to write a note of appreciation is far too time consuming. In my ministry I have noted that there are some kind people around who come to talk when they haven't a complaint and make an appointment to see me when they aren't contemplating a divorce! They are such a joy. They refresh my soul. Their generous spirit is a tonic.

When Jill and I visited a mission hospital in Niger, we were struck by the barrenness of the desert all around. Some of the missionaries had endeavored to grow flowers, to bring a little color into their lives. In our room was a simple vase with a single red flower, the first one we had seen for some time. It was fresh and sweet, and Jill, particularly, was thrilled by its simple presence. On inquiry I learned that it was the only flower that had grown on a certain bush that year. The bush had struggled for survival and had only been planted after a hole many feet deep had been dug and painstakingly filled with suitable refuse, over a long period of time, before being topped off with soil specially flown in by a returning missionary. Our hostess, after all this effort for one flower, plucked it and without a word placed it in the room of a tired visitor from America. When I asked her about it, she blushed, shrugged, and said, "If it made Jill happy, it was worth the effort."

Kindness is effort, and it is worth it. In the fellowship of believers it is specially necessary because it is a part of Spirit life.

But kindness of Spirit life must extend to the unbeliever, too. There are many motivations for ministry and numerous incentives to evangelism. None is more winsome nor effective than the loving-kindness that reaches out in genuine sympathy to the spiritually forlorn and, regardless of personal cost, generously and unstintingly communicates the reality of Christ. Kindness never leaves the spiritual babe alone, but continues to pick the sweet flowers of truth to furnish the plain room of desert living. There are no substitutes for kindness in the lives of those who know the loving-kindness of God. This is Spirit life.

In the early days of Christianity, there was some confusion among the pagans concerning the words *chrestos*, "kind," and *Christos*, "Christ," and the confusion carried over into uncertainty as to whether these strange people were followers of someone they called *Christos* or whether they had a religion based on kindness. A most fortunate point of confusion!

It is also worthwhile remembering that *chrestos* is used in the Greek translation of the Old Testament to describe "very good" figs, "precious" stones, and "pure" gold. There is something classy about kindness. It sets itself apart from other attitudes in much the same way that ripe figs differ from rotten, precious stones are worth more than cheap imitations, and pure gold is different from the dross of the dirt in which it is found.

QUESTIONS

1. What is the definition of the Hebrew word for "kindness"? How did God show kindness to Israel? What individuals in the Bible showed this sort of kindness?

2. Three attitudes show kindness. How can each be shown in daily life?
   a. sympathy
   b. benevolence
   c. generosity

7
Goodness

Good and *goodness* are two of our most popular words. We all know that evil is the opposite of good, and only the lunatic fringes of society espouse evil and despise good. There is a broad agreement that the path of goodness is the right way to go. As children we were encouraged to "do good," and in our mature years we like to think we are "doing good," and there is little disagreement that our ultimate goal is the "good life." So far, so good!

But there is a problem. For a long time now mankind has been in a debate on the subject of what constitutes goodness. This has nothing to do with being and doing good—that's a long way down the road. Before being and doing good, people must get around to defining good, and therein lies the problem.

The Goodness Debate

Those magnificent people who lived among the lemons and olives of Ancient Greece, walking and talking, discussing and debating, spent much of their time on the subject of the good life. Modern visitors to Greece think the picturesque islands, the clear skies, and the warm, fragrant air are pretty good, although the pollution that is crumbling the Parthenon, the traffic snarls in Athens, and political uncertainty spoil things a little. Many people wonder what those old-time Greek scholars had to discuss—they should have known how good things were for them—but they had difficulty deciding all the same.

Pleasure and pain

One school of thought, which has a large modern following, saw good as the experience of pleasure and the eradication of pain. This line of thinking, which has obvious attractive aspects, has led to many of our modern woes. For instance, if my pleasure is good, then anything that causes me displeasure is bad. So if my marriage is causing tension or unhappiness, I owe it to myself to get out. Divorce and desertion, in this line of reasoning, become good. If drinking to excess helps me to forget life's problems and if snorting cocaine gives me a high that won't quit, then in the pleasure they bring, goodness is found. Good then becomes that which is destroying my liver, frying my mind, and terrorizing my wife.

No one in his right mind would be in favor of inflicting pain, and most people would agree with the Greeks that the eradication of pain is good. Taken to its modern conclusion, this philosophy has produced in the Western world mammoth medical services, social services, welfare agencies, government spending, and enterprising businesses, which have done much to alleviate misery and much to produce more. Selfishness, laziness, loss of self-respect, deterioration of commitment to work, refusal to grapple with problems have followed in the wake of much well-meaning goodness, and for some segments of society real goodness has been stood on its head.

Education and ignorance

The acquisition of knowledge was touted by other Greek teachers as the goodness they were seeking. In the same way that some saw pain as evil and its eradication as good, they saw ignorance as the enemy and education as the knight on a white charger. This theory, which also has obvious merits, assumes that education will always be right and will never lead people down the garden path. It is also predicated on the belief that, having taught people what is good, they will spontaneously and joyously choose to do it. Many people who deplore ignorance and encourage education are skeptical of this ancient theory and its modern offspring. Pointing to the absence of values in modern education, the banal production of sophisticated media technology, the incidence of crime in the new echelons of cultured crooks, and the remarkable ability of our best minds to produce problems they apparently can't solve, many people are less than ecstatic about the concept of knowledge as savior and education as deliverer.

Doing unto others

Less abstract and more practical, but still suspect, is the theory that good is "doing to others what you wish them to do to you." At first sight, this theory has merit. In fact, Christ himself appeared to approve of something quite similar. The difficulty is that what we wish others to do to us may not always be good. To suggest that it will always be good is to make myself the arbiter of goodness and my own desires and aspirations the measuring criteria of all good. This is patently unsatisfactory, and even if it could be substantiated, it is clear even from the various Greek philosophies of old and the conflicting ideas of today that no consensus could be reached on what is good, and more conflict and confusion would be expected.

Greatest good for the majority

Another attractive ancient concept saw good as "the greatest benefit for the greatest number." This idea has its modern-day disciples and adherents in the structures of the great Western democracies. It allows for the fact that opinions will differ and comes down on the side of the majority. It recognizes that there are relative benefits and disadvantages for somebody in just about every situation and comes down on the side of "the most benefit." This obviously isn't so good for the minority and will be regarded as something close to evil by those who derive least benefit!

Winston Churchill, with the benefit of access to enemy codes, knew that Coventry was due to be bombed on a certain night. To evacuate the city would have saved hundreds of lives and alerted the enemy that the code had been broken. To leave the citizens of Coventry to their fiery fate would maintain access to the enemy's secrets and presumably save more lives. The decision was made to sacrifice the people of Coventry for the greater benefit of the greatest number—a decision with horrendous implications. The difficulty with this theory is that the "greatest benefit" cannot accurately be judged, and the greatest number may never be measurable. If good is defined in terms such as these, there should be no surprise at the confusing attitudes toward goodness that prevail.

Having goods and goodies

When I was preaching on this subject in my home church, I could not help noticing a number of people were granting me less than their full attention. Some told me after the service, "Far too philosophical, Stuart!" But I noticed that attention sparked when I began to speak on the next point—that "good is having goods and goodies!" I was not imagining this, because it happened in all three services, and I know that those who disdained philosophical thought were interested in a philosophy they recognized as their own. Put at its lowest level, most people define good for themselves and others in basically materialistic terms. This despite the fact that on every hand there is evidence that the material often fails to satisfy and, rather than producing good, becomes a curse and a monster.

All these ancient theories that live in our midst in modern dress contain some elements of attractive truth and in different ways attempt to address the realities of human existence. They vary widely in outlook and emphasis, but they share a common factor and accordingly suffer from a fatal flaw. They are all man-centered and are limited and condemned by their arrogant and mistaken assumption, "Man is the measure of all things."

A Criterion for Ultimate Good

Any consideration of the goodness of Spirit life, while being cognizant of man-centered concepts of goodness, must have a different point of reference, and Scripture leaves no room for doubt on the subject. Nothing could be clearer than: "For the

LORD is good and his love endures forever; his faithfulness continues through all generations" (Ps. 100:5).

The Lord Jesus, when confronted by the young man who called him good teacher, seemed a little brusque when he retorted, "Why do you call me good?" But his statement, "No one is good—except God alone," coupled with his exposure of the young man's misplaced confidence in his own goodness, showed the necessity of challenging the underlying misconceptions about goodness, even in those who are spiritual enough to ask, "What must I do to inherit eternal life?" (Mark 10:17-18). God, not man, is the measure of all things, including goodness.

This broad-based generalization is crucial to our understanding of goodness. It focuses attention on the necessity for a seeking after divine revelation rather than the all-too-common satisfaction with human rationalization. We are told in Scripture that because God is good, what he does is good. The creation narrative has a special rhythm and momentum built into its literary form. Each part of creation is described as being a result of God's command to leap into existence and, after divine scrutiny and examination, is proclaimed good. When God was finished creating, before resting, he surveyed "all that he had made, and it was very good" (Gen. 1:31). In addition, Scripture teaches that what God says is good. "Your laws are good," wrote the psalmist, adding by way of description:

How sweet are your words to my taste,
　sweeter than honey to my mouth! . . .
The unfolding of your words gives light;
　it gives understanding to the simple.
Psalms 119:39, 103, 130

The delightful honey sweetness of God's law is related to its goodness. The light that it imparts to human understanding and living is always beneficial and intrinsically good.

Furthermore, the goodness of God is translated to us through his will, which is also good. Paul assured the Roman Christians that the will of God, when adequately embraced, would prove to be "good, pleasing, and perfect" (Rom. 12:2). He also taught the grand, reassuring truth that God's involvement in human affairs is designed to bring about "the good" (Rom. 8:28). We must admit this ultimate good is not spelled out in the detail the modern pragmatic mind would desire and perhaps demand. But the focus on good being an eternal reality is crucially important, as is the emphasis that good is described in what God has said and is demonstrated in what God has done.

Good and Evil

The Christian understanding of goodness is radically different from the secular outlook. The Christian understanding finds its reality in God's goodness shown in word, work, and will. Non-believers find goodness in the idea that man in and of himself is the standard of all that is good.

Clearly, abstract ideas of good and theological statements about goodness must be translated into the language of life. Scripture accomplishes this. As we have already noted, man was pronounced "very good" by the Creator, who reserves to himself the right to define goodness. This statement does not deal with the obvious fact that people, whom God described as "very good," are sadly adept at being "very bad."

Scripture explains the saga of the "tree of the knowledge of good and evil." In all the gorgeous and varied plenty of Eden, made for God's glory and man's benefit, stood a tree. It may have stood apart from the others, either in form or location, but this need not necessarily have been the case. It may have produced special leaves and borne unique fruit, but these distinctives were not necessary to distinguish it as the tree of the knowledge of good and evil. Its one necessary distinctive was that God said it was not to be touched by Adam and Eve—that's all! But man—"very good" man—disobeyed, and the Fall fell, and immediately humankind knew good and evil. Good, we discovered too late, is knowing and doing God's good and pleasing and perfect will. Evil, we discovered—although we need never have known—is not doing God's good will.

The Battle for Goodness

Ever since Eden's tragic day, man has known with varying degrees of clarity that there is good and there is evil. He has also been aware that he himself is the battleground where the hand-to-hand fighting of the cosmic forces wages its war. If he has learned that evil needs to be forgiven and good pursued, he will have rejoiced to learn that Christ died for our sins and lives to be the One who makes available "good things" both now and hereafter (Heb. 9:11). The goodness of these good things, when properly appreciated, stimulates the grateful believer to "good works, which God prepared in advance for us to do" (Eph. 2:10).

Of course, it is not as simple as all that, because while the Holy Spirit lives in the believer to stimulate and empower to a life of obedience, the inner battle goes on. Like Paul, many people have to testify, "For I have the desire to do what is good, but I cannot carry it out. For what I do is not the good I want to do; no, the evil I do not want to do—this I keep on doing" (Rom. 7:18-19). Paul goes on to explain, however, that all is not doom and gloom. The Holy Spirit, having illuminated the benighted mind to the light and sweetness of good, continues to motivate the desires and aspirations to be and do good by God's standards. Through the indwelling power of the risen Christ, the Holy Spirit enables those of us who depend on God and who choose to obey him to do good that will not only authenticate our profession in the eyes of a watching world, but will also glorify our Father in heaven. As the Lord encouraged his disciples: "Let your light shine before men, that they may see your good deeds and praise your Father in heaven" (Matt. 5:16).

Two of the most simple, profound, practical statements concerning good come from Paul. He wrote: "Hate what is evil; cling to what is good" (Rom. 12:9), and, "Do not be overcome by evil, but overcome evil with good" (Rom. 12:21).

The most obvious evils of our society are usually quite repulsive to believers, and they hold little attraction and therefore afford little temptation. To be repelled by something gross can easily lead to hating that particular evil. But the less gross and accordingly more seductive and dangerous evils are the ones to watch. It is all too easy to relish secretly that which is wrong but respectable and to admire that which is evil but acceptable. The erosion of principle that comes from careless exposure to the attractively wrong only becomes apparent in some lives with the incidence of spiritual and moral collapse. It is learning to identify the dangerously attractive evil and disciplining oneself to hate it that is necessary for good to triumph.

But there is a positive side, too. Clinging to the good is like hanging on a rope when you're tired. It is working conscientiously when you're bored, sticking with your marriage when you're disappointed, and being committed in your church when it is not going anywhere. It is holding on through disappointment, persevering in discouragement, and pressing through disillusionment. Missionaries working with Muslims, who see little response, understand it. Mothers with retarded children do it. Ministers with truculent congregations exemplify it. Why? Because they know God's will and they choose to do it! This is a far cry from good being the presence of pleasure and the absence of pain. It may even be far removed from secular concepts of the greatest benefit for the greatest number. But it does have one feature that transcends all other considerations: It is God's will. And that means it is worth clinging to, whatever else may happen.

When we come to Paul's second piece of instruction, we are immediately reminded that hating and putting some distance between ourselves and evil is only one response. The other is to "overcome" evil, and the weapon to be used is "good." There is an unfortunate emphasis in Christian circles that take evil seriously on the importance of not being overcome, without the balancing emphasis of the necessity of doing some overcoming. The ongoing battle of good and evil requires both defensive and offensive postures.

Barnabas, whom Luke describes simply as "a good man, full of the Holy Spirit and faith" (Acts 11:24), beautifully illustrates this. When Saul of Tarsus professed faith in Christ and attempted to align himself with the church in Jerusalem, there was considerable resistance. Undoubtedly Saul's record of opposition and persecution was as well-known as it was formidable. But the attitude of exclusivism, which owed much to paranoid prejudice, was hardly an adornment of the gospel of the Christ who had given such a broad invitation to all who wished to come and had mandated an outreach to all the world. Barnabas would have none of this and with great courage, grace, and tact turned around the opinion of the church, and the renegade they nearly rejected was preserved to become the apostle they learned to revere.

Later when this same Saul, now Paul, reacted vehemently to the failure of young John Mark to exhibit the maturity expected by the apostle, Barnabas, resisting the angry short-sightedness of Paul, insisted the boy be given another chance. The apostle refused, so Barnabas parted company with Paul, took Mark with him, and preserved for the church the run-away youth who was to become not only a gospel author, but also someone prized by Paul himself.

It would have been easy for Barnabas not to bother with such tiresome and troublesome matters, but he wasn't committed to the good life of ease, comfort, and popularity. His commitment was to goodness, found in doing the will of God from the heart and in so doing overcoming the evil rampant on every hand.

There is a clear-cut need for good people who will live good lives in situations that may not always encourage them and in a society that may not always appreciate them. But the clarion call has been sounded, and the time for decision has come. Which definition of goodness do we accept—the human-centered or the God-centered? Whose side are we on—good or evil? What aspirations do we cherish—the "good life" now or the "well done, good and faithful servant" later?

The answers are important because Spirit life includes goodness, and goodness doesn't come naturally; it always requires a decision.

QUESTIONS

1. Describe five Greek philosophies concerning goodness. Why aren't they sufficient for determining what is good?

2. How can the ultimate good be determined?

3. What is the battleground for the fight between good and evil? How does this affect the Christian walk? What part does the Holy Spirit play in this battle?

4. What two statements did Paul make concerning good? How do these influence your Christian life?

8
Faithfulness

Faithfulness is not a common word. We use it at silver wedding anniversaries, when we thank our tearful wives for "twenty-five wonderful years of faithful, loving support," or as we present a gold watch to a man who is leaving the office after a lifetime behind the same desk, or as we take our old, faithful dog to the vet for the last time. But that just about covers the waterfront.

Perhaps the word is not common in our modern world because we don't need it so much anymore. Twenty-five-year marriages have become a rarity simply because they require faithfulness to a commitment. And employer-employee relationships are such that lifetime service in one company is about as common as handwritten ledgers and steam locomotives. The commitment to personal happiness, personal gain, and corporate profit has, to a large extent, pushed faithfulness so far into the background that it is legitimate to ask whether we still understand what the word means. Yet, ironically, faithfulness is so common that the seeing eye can observe it at any given moment in any given situation.

Faithfulness is an integral part of human existence, so important that without it society would disintegrate. In Chicago in the fall of 1982, a number of people were wrong when they assumed that the list of ingredients was accurate on the packet of Extra-Strength Tylenol. They assumed the faithfulness of the statement, trusted it implicitly, and died of cyanide poisoning. That which they had believed contained healing properties was in fact laced with deadly destruction. They, like millions of other purchasers of materials in stores around the world, quite reasonably believed that what was advertised was true, that what they were told was correct, and that if they paid their money, they would receive what they expected. This requires all manner of trust and all kinds of reliable, truthful, faithful service. Without it commerce would not work, as is shown clearly by the mountains of legislation that have accumulated over the years to ensure that faithfulness in advertising, marketing, contracting, banking, and investing is scrupulously adhered to. It was a great shock to consumers to discover the possibility of cyanide in the capsules. Immediately sales of certain products dropped dramatically, and people began peering suspiciously at every capsule and pill within twenty feet. This in itself showed how much we take faithfulness for granted.

Faithfulness is important to human well-being because humans were made to operate on the principle of faith. We inhabit a planet suspended without visible means of support, spinning in vast space, in a silence eerie and unbroken. There is nothing we can do to perpetuate this necessary spinning and nothing we could do to fix it if it started to go wrong. We are, in other words, totally dependent for our survival.

Every morning of our lives demands an eye-opening act of faith, which rushes us into a series of trusting actions and dependent attitudes. We embark on hours of breathing air we cannot see (most of the time), eating food we have not examined, keeping appointments with people we trust to be there, passing through traffic lights we assume will prevent accidents, boarding planes we trust will stay up till they are meant to come down. Truly we live by faith because we were created to operate in the environment of dependence as surely as fish were made for water and man was made for land.

But faith requires faithfulness, or it will produce only disaster. The standoff of the superpowers, the military buildup, the mad stockpiling of nuclear arms to the equivalent of 3.5 tons of TNT for every person alive on the earth all speak of lack of faith because of the perceptions of lack of faithfulness. Trust Tylenol and get cyanide, trust a banker and get a crook, trust a politician and get a bomb, trust a boss and get a pink slip, trust an employee and get a thief, trust a husband and get a drunk, and your faith will soon demonstrate the importance of faithfulness and the disaster of faithlessness.

The Faithfulness of God

The Greek language dramatically points out the remarkable integration of faith and faithfulness. Only one word, *pistis*, is used to describe both. That is why some translations of the Bible list "faith" as part of the fruit of the Spirit, and others say "faithfulness." Personally I see no need to distinguish between the two, because faith is so dependent on faithfulness and vice versa.

When we start to consider faithfulness, our starting point must be God himself. Peter speaks of him as the "faithful Creator" to whom we need to commit ourselves, particularly when we "suffer according to God's will" (1 Pet. 4:19).

The troubled people to whom Peter wrote must have wondered why so often suffering and Christianity arrived on the scene hand in hand. But they were encouraged to trust God even when they were still hurting from their suffering and perhaps still perplexed about the role God was playing. This was easier said than done, of course, but Peter compellingly encouraged them to trust the God who is the Creator. They knew that however dark their days might be, the sun would rise and set on time. Whatever problems arose, they knew there would be air to breathe. There would always be food to eat because of the miracle of reproduction. And they could count on the support of loving friends and family in their deepest distress. All these things were guaranteed to arrive on their doorstep daily, packaged and delivered by a faithful Creator.

In this knowledge of the faithfulness of God shown in creation, the believers of Peter's era saw grounds for dependence even in the darkest of circumstances. His faithfulness stimulated their faith, and they lived by it. Probably Peter was thinking of the prophet Jeremiah speaking from the pit of discouragement:

> Because of the LORD's great love
>> we are not consumed,
>> for his compassions never fail.
> They are new every morning;
>> great is your faithfulness.
> *Lamentations 3:22-23*

God's faithfulness is also seen in the way he calls people. His invitation offers marvelous things to those who will respond. His faithfulness is seen in the way he delivers what he promises. Lots of people have been encouraged to go to swanky hotels to partake of a free dinner that cost them only an hour's attention to a smooth presentation concerning condominiums in some exotic place. At least that's what they thought it would cost them, until they found they had signed up to buy a property they could no more use than afford.

When they finally could afford the trip to see what they had bought, they found they had been taken! But God's offer, call, or invitation is linked to his faithfulness because he is as capable as he is willing to give his children what he promised he would give. And his faithfulness is guaranteed in that he always means what he says and says what he means. The significance of this is clearly shown by such statements as: "He will keep you strong to the end, so that you will be blameless on the day of our Lord Jesus Christ" (1 Cor. 1:8).

A promise of such dimensions stirs the most exhilarating hope in the human heart, but hope has its doubts, and sooner or later a little voice will ask, "But how can I be sure he *will* keep me?" The answer is, "God, who has called you into fellowship with his son Jesus Christ our Lord, is faithful" (1 Cor. 1:9). The faith that breeds assurance is rooted in the faithfulness of a God who cannot lie and who must always be true to himself.

The ultimate experience of our salvation is laid up in heaven for us, guaranteed by the faithful God. But the immediate experience has many hard edges. These hard edges are no surprise to the Lord; in fact, he permits them for a purpose. We look at them as temptations, but from his angle they are tests. He sees them as opportunities to do right, but sadly we see them as chances to go wrong. In the divine way of looking at things, these pressures are potentially productive, but from under the pressure it is hard to see how they can be anything but totally destructive. Yet the Lord, in his wisdom, not only allows such things to happen to us, but seems to be enthusiastically in favor of them. The more mature we grow in Christ, the more sensitive we become to the possibilities of failure. As we appreciate more and more the potential for both good and evil in the day-to-day circumstances of life we look for an anchor for our souls and a point of reference to maintain our equilibrium. Both are found in the Lord, who, as Paul writes "is faithful; he will not let you be tempted beyond what you can bear. But when you are tempted, he will also provide a way out so that you can stand up under it" (1 Cor. 10:13).

God's commitment to his tested people is, first, that they will not be given more than they can handle; and second, he will always build in a safety valve, so they will not burst their boilers. "But," say those who are undergoing the pressurizing, "how can I know this is true?" The answer: "God is faithful."

A few days ago a distressed lady asked to talk with me about a matter of importance. She was very young, strikingly beautiful, and distraught. Her sad story of deception and disgrace moved her to tears, and my heart was heavy, not only for her and the others involved, but also for a society in which such things are becoming commonplace. Eventually she asked me, "Is there any hope for me? Can I ever lose my sense of shame? Is God prepared to forgive?"

I gladly told her of the free gift of grace, but carefully pointed out to her that the forgiveness, which is without cost to us, cost Christ everything.

This, she said, was the most beautiful thing she had ever heard, but then she added, "But how can I be sure that all is forgiven?"

"Because of what God's Word says," I replied. " 'If we confess our sins, he is faithful and just and will forgive us our sins and purify us from all unrighteousness' " (1 John 1:9).

After a time of confession and supplication, our prayers turned to adoration as she laid hold of the wonder of forgiveness guaranteed in God's faithfulness.

One of life's greatest treasures is the knowledge that with God there is no false advertising, no deceptive business practices, no broken contracts. He is utterly faithful. Upon this we can build lives set upon the rock; without this we have only sinking sand.

Faithfulness with Faith

But faithfulness without faith is like a checking account without checks. It takes faith's check to release the values of the checking account's faithfulness. Without faith, faithfulness lies in the vaults of life, gathering dust. This is why faith is built into the fiber of man's experience. It is God's way of allowing man to experience and exhibit God's faithfulness.

So the man who wakes each morning at the crack of dawn (or noon) with a recognition of God and an acknowledgment of the "new mercies" releases a knowledge of God's faithfulness as the one who creates. When he trusts God to lead him unerringly through a maze of possible mistakes, he exhibits a sense of God's faithfulness as the one who calls to eventual glory.

In the same way, dependence, both humble and optimistic, in God's protecting and governing hand in the middle of unspeakable adversity proves to men of faith God's faithfulness as the one who controls our destiny. And as the young lady who found relief in Christ's promise of forgiveness discovered, faith that trusts God to forgive sin shows his faithfulness as the one who cleanses.

In what way is this related to Spirit life? It is the Spirit who opens our eyes to Scripture as it states God's faithfulness. The Holy Spirit brings to our minds and hearts a clear understanding of our needs that necessitate the benefits his faithfulness provides. And it is the Holy Spirit who, working in ways beyond our comprehension, stimulates us to responses of faith, expressions of trust, and exclamations of praise based on God's faithfulness.

Intellectual belief

But now we need to turn our attention to faith. Faith is spoken of in different ways; it shows itself in many forms. In some ways it is an exercise of the intellect. For instance, we intellectually "believe that Jesus is the Christ" because we have assembled data concerning him, his claims, his miracles, his death and resurrection and have concluded that he is who he claims to be. To believe that something is true is intellectual.

Believing in

We are also required to believe "in" or to "believe God." This takes us past the intellectual into the relational aspect of faith. Here facts concerning a person give way to the Person. The cold, hard edges of truth are smoothed in the warm, rounded embrace of trust and trustworthiness. Knowing that Christ is true expands to knowing Christ is real.

Believing on

"Believing on" is yet another term for faith that suggests the part played by choice. It has the ring of commitment, the drama of decision. It is faith making a move, changing a position, adopting a stance, standing up to be seen and counted. It is Noah taking a deep breath and boarding his mammoth boat before the mocking faces of his contemporaries and bracing himself on the solid deck. It is Daniel, innocent and abused, refusing to compromise and facing down those who would destroy that for which he lives. Believing on the Lord Jesus will lead a worker to defy his union and be called a scab because of conviction. It will move a young girl to decline a proposal from the one she loves because he does not share a commitment to the One she loves more.

But faith once initiated must be perpetuated. The original act of faith needs to be perpetuated in acts and attitudes of faith described by the apostle Paul as "walking by faith." This experience, which is absolutely vital to spiritual experience, is not necessary for the salvation of our souls but is crucial to the saving of our lives. Faith in the Lord's direction, trust in his Word, obedience to his commands, and dependence upon his power are the ingredients of the life of faith. Without these things there is no sense of being on track, and invariably those who try to operate without walking by faith find themselves confused and befuddled by all manner of ideas and all kinds of approaches to life. They listen to friends whose knowledge of God may be, at best, limited, and at worst, negligible. They imbibe attitudes from soap operas and develop strategies from best-sellers and often protest loudly the fact that they have been "saved," even though their lives lie in ironic ruins.

Scripture teaches that we walk by faith, live by faith, stand by faith, pray in faith, and overcome through faith, in addition to being saved by faith, so it stands to reason that any life not operating by faith will be shaky in all these areas. But the believer living and walking by faith lives in the daily enjoyment of God's faithfulness and relishes the ceaseless provision of his every need.

Three Forms of Faithfulness

Faith and faithfulness need each other like keys and locks. The lock has the ability to show that the key is right, and the key has what it takes to show what the lock can do. Keys without locks may be ornamental, but nothing else. Locks without keys are useless at best, and can be infuriating, depending on where you left the key and whether the door was locked!

In the same way, faith demonstrates that faithfulness is for real, and faithfulness invites and encourages faith's ongoing participation.

But there is a further aspect to the relationship between the two. Men and women of faith know the importance of faithfulness not only as the ground of faith, but also as its product. As surely as faithfulness stimulates faith, faith produces faithfulness. Those who exercise faith revel in the solid response of faithfulness to their trust, but they also endeavor to provide a trustworthy example to a world deficient in a model of faithfulness. This kind of faithful behavior, the product of faith, is also part of Spirit life.

Faithfulness when persecuted

The Lord pulled no punches when he told the disciples that they would have trouble in the world. He made no concessions and offered them no escape, but he did promise to be with them. They were trained with the knowledge that they were enrolled in a conflict of cosmic proportions. Their enemies were not flesh and blood, but spiritual, powerful, and utterly evil. In practical terms this meant a great amount of physical abuse and appalling danger, sometimes even leading to martyrdom. It is not insignificant that the Greek word for "witness" is *martus*—a connection that never let the disciples forget that martyrs are witnesses who meet hostility in its most aggressive form, and witnesses are people who know that their calling can include occupational hazards of fearsome magnitude.

The apostles, in their letters to the churches of the first century, developed the theme of persecution, some of them even writing the story in their own blood. But always they reminded the believers of the privilege of suffering for the One who suffered the ultimate; of the unlimited resources of resolve and courage in the Holy Spirit, the Word, and the believing community; and of the necessity for faithfulness— perseverance in persuasion while under pressure. The believers in Smyrna were told by the Lord, through John:

Do not be afraid of what you are about to suffer. I tell you, the devil will put some of you in prison to test you, and you will suffer persecution for ten days. Be faithful, even to the point of death, and I will give you the crown of life.
Revelation 2:10

Believers, young and old, were confronted with the choice of denying Christ and living, or affirming Christ and dying. To be faithful under those conditions was to die. Sometimes the choice was not as clear-cut: Simply acknowledge Caesar and keep your religion, and we won't bother you so long as you show your patriotism in your submission to the authorities. To be faithful in those days was to refuse to bow to Caesar as Lord, lest it should reflect on the conviction that Christ alone is Lord. This was treason in the eyes of the law, and the faithful were faithful unto death.

Those days and issues may appear far removed from our contemporary situations, but the appearance is deceptive. Not many years ago Korean believers laid their commitments on the line and their blood in the sand. Ugandan believers took a stand against anything that might compromise their position. Central American countries in the ferment of revolution have lost many of their sons and daughters out of solid, unflinching commitment, and Ethiopian Christians in great numbers have refused to bow to Marxist demands that contravene Christian conviction. Their suffering has shown faithfulness in its most glowing colors.

Living, as many of us do, in less hostile and more amenable circumstances, faithfulness unto death may seem an extreme possibility, but faithfulness unto life faces us all in a dozen choices.

Faithfulness to doctrinal purity

Doctrinal purity was another concern of the early believers, and to them faithfulness meant a tenacious treasuring of the truth. Writing to his friend and fellow believer Gaius, John was most complimentary:

> It gave me great joy to have some brothers come and tell about your faithfulness to the truth and how you continue to walk in the truth. I have no greater joy than to hear that my children are walking in the truth.
> *3 John 3-4*

Twenty centuries after Christ's time on earth we have become accustomed to the broad sweep of Christian theology, modern criticisms, and attempted revisions of it and what we regard as the fundamentals of the faith. But in the formative years of the church, many issues concerning the nature and deity of Christ, the means of grace, and Christian ethics were being fiercely debated. People from a Jewish background clearly struggled with the concept of a suffering Messiah instead of a charismatic, popular hero-deliverer. Others from a Greek background, which stressed the evilness of matter, were appalled at the suggestion that God should assume bodily form. Numerous theological differences arose. Judaism on the one hand was making powerful attacks on the infant church, while Gnosticism attacked on a different but no less powerful front. And in the middle stood believers committed to the truth delivered to them through the apostles. These teachers were not intimidated by their opponents and waged serious war against every threat to their gospel. Paul showed the strength of their feelings when he told the Galatians: "As we have already said, so now I say again: If anybody is preaching to you a gospel other than what you accepted, let him be eternally condemned!" (Gal. 1:9).

The apostles were playing hardball when it came to their proclamation and defense of the truth, and they expected the believers to be able to recognize truth from error and embrace the one and shun the other. To them this was the essence of faithfulness.

In the name of "faithfulness to the truth" great battles have continued to rage down through the Christian centuries. Some have been inexcusable in their cruel use of force, others less than laudable in their ability to swallow theological camels and gag on ecclesiastical gnats. Bellicose believers have always been able to find a Bible brawl somewhere, and some preachers have built a ministry on rounding up such "faithful" souls and leading them into the fray. This approach has been so distasteful to many of God's people that they have shunned every issue and surrendered truth's high ground without even offering token resistance. To the "belligerent faithful" Paul would say, as he did to Timothy:

119

Don't have anything to do with foolish and stupid arguments, because you know they produce quarrels. And the Lord's servant must not quarrel; instead, he must be kind to everyone, able to teach, not resentful.
2 Timothy 2:23-24

But the benign noncombatants need to remember Jude's robust challenge: "I had to write and urge you to contend for the faith that was once for all entrusted to the saints" (Jude 3).

Because of the differing opinions among convinced believers on such matters as the nature of inspiration and authority, the details of eschatology, social responsibility and ecumenicity, a correct stance on faithfulness to the truth is not always easy to identify or maintain. But the necessity for spiritual insight and maturity in such matters is clearly stated by the inclusion of faithfulness in Spirit life.

Faithfulness to others

There is another aspect of faithfulness closely related to the two we have discussed above. Gaius also exhibited it, and John explained it as follows: "You are faithful in what you are doing for the brothers, even though they are strangers to you" (3 John 5).

Presumably "the brothers" in question were engaging in some kind of itinerant ministry where they were to some extent dependent on the hospitality of the believers. Diotrophes, who was on some kind of leadership ego trip, didn't want them around. Gaius did, took them in, and generously cared for them. His faithfulness came through as a ruggedly reliable sense of responsibility. Paul also looked for this kind of people and advised Timothy to concentrate his teaching ministry on "faithful men . . . able to teach others also" (2 Tim. 2:2, KJV).

Few things delight me more than working with reliable people, and few experiences are more disappointing than being let down! The writer of Proverbs said it all: "Like a bad tooth or a lame foot is reliance on the unfaithful in times of trouble" (Prov. 25:19).

But Paul reminded the Corinthians, who were not known for their reliability, "Those who have been given a trust must prove faithful" (1 Cor. 4:2), and there is no doubt that those who trust the faithful God are trusted by the faithful God—to be faithful!

QUESTIONS

1. Why is faithfulness an important part of Spirit life? What is the believer's basis for faithfulness?

2. How does Scripture describe God's faithfulness? How does the Christian experience this faithfulness? What is the Holy Spirit's role in this aspect of the fruit?

3. Name three forms of faith. How are these perpetuated in the Christian experience?

4. What problems concerning faith did the first-century church face? How did they overcome them?

9
Meekness

Robert Ringer wrote a book called *Looking Out for No. 1*, which became a best-seller. This was a surprise to me, because most people I have met could probably have written it and hardly needed to read it! Along the same wavelength he produced *Winning Through Intimidation*, a book widely acclaimed and even more widely practiced. Meanwhile back in the church, preachers were still plodding on with "the meek shall inherit the earth" while many of their sheep either listened politely or said, "You've got to be kidding!" Warming to his theme, Ringer then came out with *Restoring the American Dream*, and suddenly to propagate meekness became practically un-American in addition to being "impractical," "naive," and "stupid." Unfortunately, the word *meekness* suffers because it rhymes with *weakness*, and the two have become synonymous in people's minds. Even believers have been heard to say, "Who needs this meekness stuff? I'm not weak, and I'm not about to pretend I am!" Ironically, meekness in its true form is far from weakness, because to be properly exhibited it requires unusual strength.

Understanding the Meaning of Meekness

Praotes is the word used by Paul in "the fruit of the Spirit" list. It was a word with which Greeks were familiar, particularly those who had a working knowledge of Aristotle. He had a theory that a virtue is the mean between two vices. Rage was a vice that reigned supreme at one end of the personality; indifference was found at the opposite extreme. Planted firmly in between, and therefore qualifying as a virtue in Aristotle's book, was *praotes*—meekness. The finest example of meekness in his eyes was portrayed by Socrates as he was presented with the poison and required to drink. Others who had suffered such a fate had raged at their opponents, called down destruction on their tormentors, and generally behaved in the way that might be expected. Socrates, to the amazement of the onlookers, did no such thing. It would be natural to assume that perhaps Socrates was simply indifferent to his fate and was shrugging his shoulders as he sipped his hemlock. But this was not the case as the dying man began to speak to all those within earshot about the things that concerned him. To refuse to rage and to avoid being indifferent in such circumstances was the epitome of *meekness* and it quite clearly had no similarity whatsoever to *weakness*. It was Socratic strength, which was capable of control in circumstances beyond his control, that Aristotle spoke of so warmly.

Meekness in the Scriptures

Scripture gives us even more clear pictures of meekness in the lives of such people as Moses, Paul, and our Lord. Moses is called "more humble [meek] than anyone else on the face of the earth" (Num. 12:3). Now we know that Moses was far from perfect; he killed an Egyptian and buried him in the sand; he argued with God about going to Pharaoh; he got fed up with his grumbling congregation in the wilderness, took his frustrations out on a rock, and got himself banned from the Holy Land. But he was wonderfully strong when it came to meekness. His brother and sister, Aaron and Miriam, gave him a hard time concerning his wife. There was nothing unusual about that, of course: it was just normal sibling bickering! But things got past that stage, and Aaron and Miriam began to show unseemly pride in their own status and achievements and less than proper respect for their brother-leader. This was not acceptable to the Lord, and he called all three before him and addressed Aaron and Miriam in a few well-chosen words:

"When a prophet of the Lord is among you,
I reveal myself to him in visions,
I speak to him in dreams.
But this is not true of my servant Moses;
he is faithful in all my house.
With him I speak face to face,
clearly and not in riddles;
he sees the form of the LORD.
Why then were you not afraid
to speak against my servant Moses?"

Numbers 12:6-8

Moses showed mildness in the face of opposition and criticism. He could have reminded his brother and sister that they owed their position to him. He could have pointed out the clear superiority of his position and presumably could have encouraged them to shut up or ship out. Moses chose to show great strength and reserve instead. He held his peace. Apparently

Moses made no attempt to explain his unique status with God. In fact, we would never have known about it if God himself had not taken Moses' critics to one side and set the record straight. It takes a certain kind of restraint and strength to refuse to brag, to live humbly with honor, and to choose not to use weapons of defense that would blow the opposition out of the water.

But Moses' gentleness and meekness were most beautifully shown in his reaction to Miriam's leprosy. She had been particularly critical of Moses' wife from Cush—a black lady in all probability. So God judged her by giving a special treatment: "there stood Miriam—leprous, like snow" (Num. 12:10). A very white treatment for a lady objecting to a black in-law! But Moses, horrified, cried out to the Lord, "O God, please heal her!" (Num. 12:13).

Some people need to toot their own horns, bang their drums, wave their credentials, recount their exploits, polish their egos, and guard their territory—that's weakness. Others have done exploits, achieved successes, been granted honors, and scaled the heights, but find no necessity to inform those who are ignorant or remind those who are conversant—that's meekness.

The place of meekness in Spirit life is explained by the Lord himself in well-known words:

"Come to me, all you who are weary and burdened, and I will give you rest. Take my yoke upon you and learn from me, for I am gentle and humble in heart."
Matthew 11:28-29

Meekness, being part of the nature of Christ, becomes a learning experience for his disciples as they are yoked to him. Not only does the life of Christ model meekness, but commitment to him enables disciples to develop it in their lives. In much the same way that the Eastern farmer lays the heavy wooden yoke over the shoulder of both the old ox and the young one in order that they might walk and work in step, so the Lord teaches meekness one step at a time to those who walk with him.

The classic example that our Lord gave for our learning was on the day of his triumphal entry into Jerusalem. Matthew, using the words of the prophet, exclaimed:

"Say to the Daughter of Zion,
  'See your king comes to you,
gentle and riding on a donkey,
    on a colt, the foal of a donkey.' "
Matthew 21:5

The word translated "gentle" in both these passages from Matthew is *praotes*, "meekness." The most casual observer in the crowds greeting the Son of David—a royal title—on that day could not fail to notice his royal mount was a young, unbroken colt. Jesus certainly was not trying to impress anyone! Once again he was showing that the kingdom he had come to establish would not be based on winning through intimidation, and by no stretch of the imagination could he be accused of looking out for Number One! Self-denial, not self-assertion, was the philosophy of his life. Self-effacement, not self-promotion, sets the tone for his behavior. Jesus had nothing to prove, no one to impress. His Father was in control, and he was content to leave the glory to him. Even the adoring crowds and the rapturous cheers that in a few days would turn to rancorous jeers did not excite him into grandiose statements and melodramatic gestures. Quietly and consistently Christ made his humble, meek way through the crowds and did what he needed to do. That was not weakness; it was meekness.

The strength of meekness is hidden to many eyes by what they perceive as spineless submissiveness. But careful evaluation of Moses and Christ, not to mention Socrates and Paul, shows that they were submissive not because they were spineless, but because they chose to be strong. It came as the result of a conscious decision not to be assertive. No doubt all of them were tempted to stand up for what was their right and on occasion felt that they were neither adequately understood nor appreciated. But meekness meant they were strong enough to choose not to make a fuss or create a scene. They were all perfectly capable of making an issue—Moses with the Egyptian, Christ in the Temple, Paul with the Athenians. They were strong, but used their strength willingly to submit to that which was less than their right and to accept much less than their due.

Meekness and the Contemporary Believer

For the contemporary believer this kind of Spirit life is particularly challenging because it is so foreign to the modern mind and flies in the teeth of modern thought. But there are a number of areas in which it is crucial that meekness be the watchword.

Meekness under the Word of God

James wrote that you should "humbly [*praotes*] accept the word planted in you, which can save you" (James 1:21). The Word of God is like a two-edged sword sometimes, a hammer other times, and has been known to be bitter to our taste. We tend to react to the authoritative Word; we don't like it when it makes us uncomfortable. We tend to become angry, sometimes at the church, other times at the preacher; but if both are doing their jobs, our irritation is really at the Word of God.

But we are instructed to receive God's Word with meekness. This does not mean we treat it with indifference, of course. We must feel free to react reverently to it; we are perfectly free to question what it says openly and unashamedly, but with the willingness to submit to its final authority in our lives once its intent is clear.

Meekness in Christian testimony

Then there is the matter of Christian testimony. The impact of Christian witness is directly related to what we have to say and the way we get around to saying it. We must not forget that our Lord was "full of grace and truth," while his followers have been known to pack plenty of truth, but little grace, and his opponents are often strong on grace, but weak in truth. Peter tied the two together when he wrote: "Always be prepared to give an answer to everyone who asks you to give the reason for the hope that you have. But do this with gentleness and respect" (1 Pet. 3:15).

Any presentation of the reason for Christian hope must include a statement concerning the basis of that hope, which is God's amazing grace. If there's one thing that grace, rightly understood, can do for a person, it is to teach meekness and humility. The whole point of grace is that it finds its roots in God and reaches out to the most undeserving and ungrateful. Whenever I speak of the reasons for hope, I point away from myself and toward the Lord of grace. That in itself is meekness, because whenever I'm asked to give my reasons for anything, there is always the possibility I might give myself all the glory. But meekness resists that impulse and glorifies God.

Meekness in attitude toward the hearer is important, too. Religion, like politics, is a highly controversial subject, and the Christian need never be far from a controversy. All he has to do is start talking about the Lord to people who don't want to know! But what about those who do want to know, those who ask for a reason? It is not uncommon to find such people reacting to what is being said, even though they asked for it. At that time meekness comes into play because there is no profit in getting into an argument. If you win an argument, you humiliate someone and lose a contact; if you lose, you feel stupid, and they lose respect for you. The experienced witness to Christ strives to keep a gentle, humble spirit as he winsomely but honestly speaks the truth in love. I can think with shame of many occasions when I spoke the truth with something less than meekness, but on other occasions I can remember how people were helped because I was happy to concede a point they made, accept criticism they voiced, or admit that I didn't know the answer to a penetrating question they asked.

Meekness in ministry

The apostle Paul, who often showed that he was no pussycat, was nevertheless anxious to show meekness in his ministry and to encourage it among those who were trying to establish the churches in pagan society. When he wrote to the Corinthians, who in many ways were his problem children, he appealed to them "By the meekness and gentleness of Christ" (2 Cor. 10:1).

Paul made it quite clear that he could come among them like a whirlwind and let them feel the sharp edge of his tongue and see the tough side of his character as he tried to set right all that was wrong at Corinth. But he hoped this would not be necessary. His fondest dream was that he could share in their fellowship in a gentle way in which they would accept his apostolic authority without question, respond to his directives without argument, and get themselves in line with what the Spirit was saying to the churches. If the Corinthians responded this way, it would not be necessary for Paul to carry a big stick or to mete out strong medicine. There would be no need for him to restate his position or to demand their cooperation. There was no doubt that Paul much preferred this approach because, having learned meekness from his Lord, he wanted to exemplify it in Christ's church. In the same way he stressed that the same attitude be demonstrated in all segments of the church as they grappled with the issues that threatened their existence and testimony.

Meekness in manner

There were controversies in abundance in Corinth; grounds for disagreement abounded, and belligerent, opinionated believers could have a field day in the community of the redeemed. But this was a luxury they could not afford. Their enemies were so powerful that they could not allow them-selves to be divided, or they might end up being conquered. They must "hang in there" together, but this would require phenomenal reserves of meekness as they confronted the issues and squared off against each other. The same is still true today.

Many a church has split on an issue, not because it was so important in the long term, but because the protagonists were so determined in the short term. The issue became clouded in the rhetoric; the things that really mattered became lost in the clash of egos and the need of some people to assert themselves and win their battles. Men have been able to claim great victories for truth and righteousness, but the pile of church rubble on which they stand to wave their triumphant flags suggests that perhaps a little more meekness and a lot less belligerence would have solved the problem without the necessity of destroying the fellowship. Meekness in manners is clearly a spiritual grace, an evidence of Spirit life.

Meekness in marriage

In light of the scandal of contemporary marital breakdown and the impact of much modern thought on the behavior patterns of married couples, great care should be taken to ensure that believers are aware of what it means to live in marriage as God would have us live. When Peter wrote his famous words about wives being submissive to their husbands and concentrating on "the unfading beauty of a gentle and quiet spirit, which is of great worth in God's sight" (1 Pet. 3:4), he could hardly have expected the uproar that would greet his words in the latter part of the twentieth century. Of course, Peter could reasonably have expected his words to be read in context, but as all writers and speakers know, this can be a little too much to expect. However, Peter's insistence on meekness on the part of wives in marital situations can only be properly understood in the light of his full treatment of the subject. Starting with the meekness and sacrificial spirit of Christ, Peter shows that without such an attitude on the part of our Lord, there would be no redemption for us.

A self-assertive Christ would never have tolerated crucifixion; all he had to do was summon the legions of angels, and the book on winning by intimidation would have needed rewriting. But he carefully used his strength for the blessing of humankind rather than self-preservation. "In the same way," Peter writes, "wives . . . be submissive" (1 Pet. 3:1). But note carefully that he also writes, "in the same way" to husbands before telling them about the consideration they must show their wives and the respect for their well-being that must characterize their marital relationships. The "in the same way" phrase links the instructions to husbands and wives with the behavior of the crucified Lord.

The crucifixion attitude should work through to the living rooms and the bedrooms of modern homes as believers recognize that meekness is fundamental to married bliss. This kind of talk is light years away from the popular modern myth of macho man and is just as far removed from contemporary insistence on the assertive woman. Women who are prepared to take steps toward meekness in marital relations will be prepared, however hard it may be, to think in terms of trading some assertiveness for helpfulness and putting on hold their newly discovered rights in order that they may fulfill an ancient responsibility.

But before the howls of protest become deafening, let me hasten to add that meekness in marriage for men must also be in evidence. For as surely as Christ left an example for women, he left one for men. Ironically, we don't hear too much about this. Perhaps because most of the preachers are men! Nevertheless a husband needs to be hanging up a lot of his macho nonsense with his worn-out jogging suits and stacking his male image in the corner of his closet with his out-of-date pants.

Then we may turn the tide on marital breakdown and see marriages where the strength of the participants is directed to building each other up instead of beating each other down. Yelling matches will give way to listening sessions; name calling will be superseded by attempts at caring and under-standing; and insistence on rights being met and needs being fulfilled will be banished forever in place of responsibilities being gladly accepted and mutual sharing becoming the pre-vailing attitude. Meekness in marriage will work wonders, and this should come as no surprise, because it has always been God's way of doing things.

Meekness in Christian leadership

One of the most challenging areas of my life is that of Chris-tian leadership. As the senior pastor of a large church, I am expected to give some kind of leadership to the congregation. My problem is not so much one of organizational structures of leadership, because I have no difficulty accepting the need for shared responsibility, clear delegation, and plurality of leadership. My problem is more related to style of leadership. There is no doubt that people's expectations of a leader vary dramatically. Some want a leader who will tell them what to do, when to do it, and no questions asked. Others don't want anybody telling them anything. There are some leaders who insist that we lead by example and others who insist that example isn't enough, that directives have to be given, ac-countability established, and heads made to roll, if necessary. There are those who point to the picture of the shepherd as one who leads the sheep, but always with a delicate touch. At the same time there are leaders who point with some degree of enthusiasm to the apostles, who never seemed to worry about wading into situations with great gusto and formidable strength of purpose.

The epistles have quite a lot to say about the place of meekness in ministry, particularly in leadership. As we have already noted, the apostle Paul, in his dealings with the church at Corinth, found it necessary to issue rebukes concerning unacceptable behavior. This is all part of the ministry in today's church—not a particularly popular part. We now have a generation of people in church who have never been subjected to much discipline since they were children. Their school days were not exactly strict, and their philosophy of life has borrowed freely from attitudes far removed from the principles of rugged discipleship. Accordingly they are quite happy to engage in life-styles that suit them, and they are greatly surprised if they are confronted with the suggestion that their behavior is not appropriate for believers. Never having been corrected for some time, this is particularly hard for them to take; and from my own experience, I can testify that a rebuke, however biblical and necessary, is not always well received in the modern church. That is why this aspect of leadership has fallen by the wayside to a certain extent. There is, however, one certainty, and that is that unless the rebuke is administered by people who have earned the right to administer it, and unless it is offered in a meek spirit, there is little hope for a positive outcome.

The main objective in the ministry of rebuke is that those who are in error might be quickly restored to the truth. But for this to happen, those who are going astray have to be convinced that they *are* going astray. Then they have to be shown that there is a right way to go, and after that they need help in making the necessary decisions and encouragement in the steps they must take. Paul told the Galatians about this and explained simply: "Brothers, if someone is caught in a sin, you who are spiritual should restore him gently. But watch yourself, or you also may be tempted" (Gal. 6:1).

The gentleness or meekness on the part of the one trying to help is shown in a spirit that is understanding rather than censorious and ready to accept that he himself is not above reproach or immune from temptation. To be able to show the hurting brother or sister that you yourself struggle may work wonders. And if you are able to assure him that while there is no way you can condone his actions, which are totally out of order, you have no difficulty understanding how it could happen because you know human frailty from personal experience, then you go a long way toward achieving the desired end of restoration of life and witness. But more often than not, it takes that meekness of spirit to do the trick.

I take great delight in Paul's letters to Timothy. It all started when I was a young preacher finding help in the aged Paul's great advice to his youthful protégé. Without noticing it, the years have slipped by, and I still think of myself as somebody's Timothy and feel the need for help from the old-timer, Paul, although I am rapidly approaching elder status! Surely one of the most helpful things Paul told Timothy and all who, like me, aspire to be Paul's protégés, is:

And the Lord's servant must not quarrel; instead, he must be kind to everyone, able to teach, not resentful. Those who oppose him he must gently instruct, in the hope that God will grant them repentance leading them to a knowledge of the truth.
2 Timothy 2:24-25

There is a certain security in a leadership style that is loud and demanding that, like E. F. Hutton, makes people listen and demands and receives instant, total attention. But it is often the security of weakness. To be so in need of that kind of security is to betray a deep inner insecurity. The real strength of meekness is the readiness to be vulnerable and honest in ministry, open and ready to serve. It is to avoid the extremes of the passive indifference of noninvolvement and the raging demands of control and status. Meekness in ministry, manners, and marriage is happy to use God-given strength as a means of saying no to selfishness in its many forms. It draws on the strength of the Spirit to find resources for service when it would be more fun to be served. Meekness is the strength of backing off from a fight you could win and a point you could nail down, for the sake of the damage that would be done and the greater issues at stake.

Meekness is not weakness, neither is it easy. But like every other aspect of Spirit life, it is required and possible through obedience to those requirements and dependence on the Spirit of Christ, who was meek and lowly of heart.

QUESTIONS

1. What was the Greek's understanding of the meaning of meekness? How is this different from today's understanding of that word?

2. How is meekness shown in the Bible? What biblical figures showed this quality?

3. Why is meekness important to the Christian testimony?

4. How does grace influence meekness? How will this combination affect the hearer of a testimony?

5. In what way can meekness touch the believer's daily life? The life of the church?

10
Self-Control

Not too many years ago we used to have temperance meetings. They were designed to explain "the evils of strong drink" and were attended by an interesting mixture of concerned elderly ladies and men of indeterminate age who obviously were much the worse for drink. They listened to talks that painted dramatic and traumatic pictures of the physical and social ills of alcohol and then went on their way to a life of sobriety or a return to their former experience, which often resulted in destroyed livers and lives.

Things have changed. Now we have "drug-dependency seminars" in which similar people, slightly more modern, listen to similar talks, slightly more updated, and go to small-group experiences considerably more sophisticated. And the results have a familiar ring to them. Some find sobriety, others oblivion. Either way there is clearly a need for healthy and practical approaches to the subject of temperance. But I mean this in not quite so limited a sense as you may suspect.

The word translated "self-control" in our list of the fruit of the Spirit used to be translated "temperance" in the older versions of the Bible, and this has led some people to think that in the biblical sense "self-control" and "temperance" are the same thing. Temperance in the limited sense means learning to handle the problems related to alcohol in such a way that you are delivered from its clutches. Temperance or self-control really throws its net much wider and means to handle all that would mar our lives before God in such a way that we can be liberated to serve him in glorious freedom. The Greek word literally means "self-mastery."

The Two Ditches of Personal Freedom

In a sense, self-control involves handling freedom properly, because Paul, in his letter to the Galatians, is taking great pains to show how free believers are not to live to excess but to live in success. The Galatians, however, were encountering the problems all thinking people encounter when they survey their freedoms and note the ways in which they can be abused. Freedom is like a highway with a ditch on each side. One ditch is called legalism and the other licentiousness. Legalism limits freedom by carefully defined structures and restrictions; licentiousness celebrates freedom and encourages the enjoyment of it to the point of excess, which eventually destroys the very thing it celebrates.

A few years ago two of our church youth workers who were new believers took the high-school kids out for a typical Milwaukee evening. That meant bowling. After bowling, pizza, and for them, with pizza, beer. Being born and bred Milwaukeeans, bowling, pizza, and beer were as inseparable as baseball, hot dogs, and apple pie—not to mention Chevrolet! But some of the parents of the young people were outraged and demanded, quite understandably, that I should make a full inquiry. I spoke with the two young believers and asked what had happened, and they quite openly said that they had ordered beer and pizza, as they had done all their lives, and they added, "Apparently we have done something wrong!" At that point it would have been easy to say, "You sure did do something wrong, you boneheads. Don't you understand that when you become a Christian, you don't drink beer, you drink soda with your pizza?" But I didn't say that, because I knew they would have asked me, "Why, what's so great about Coke and Pepsi? Caffeine isn't good for the health. And what's wrong with beer? We've never been drunk in our lives, but we've had beer in our good, old German, Milwaukee homes since we were kids!"

Instead we tried to evaluate the whole subject of Christian liberty. Together we came to the conclusion that the ditch on one side of the liberty highway had the legalistic sign on it, which said, THOU SHALT NOT DRINK BEER, EVEN ONE GLASS WITH A PIZZA. But on the other side of the highway, we knew there was a ditch that had on its licentious verge the alluring sign, YOU ONLY GO 'ROUND ONCE IN LIFE, SO HIT IT WITH ALL THE GUSTO YOU CAN! Instinctively we knew that both ditches had to be avoided if liberty was to be preserved. Legalism's ditch was adding to Scripture rules that Scripture did not find necessary to stipulate. The ditch of licentiousness was in blatant opposition to Scripture's clear teaching on drunkenness and riotous living.

Having determined that a middle line was the path of liberty, we then had another thought: But what about the high-school kids? Don't we owe them an example? Could they possibly misunderstand what was happening when their leaders had beer and pizza? We had no trouble answering that one. Of course, there was a heavy demand for a model. Naturally, high-school kids could be counted on to misunderstand whatever was done or said. Without a doubt, these kids had enough problems with their drunken and doped-up peers without having added pressure from their leaders' examples.

At that point my two young friends said, "We have the freedom to have our drink with our pizza. No one has the freedom to deny our freedom in this matter. But we have no freedom to drink to excess, which we have never done anyway. We have a responsibility to the kids, so we will not touch another glass of beer in their presence." As a result, the two leaders asked to address the high-school group at the next meeting, explained their position, apologized for any confusion, and stated their decision, explaining that they were freely choosing to exercise self-control in the area of freedom, not because of any rules, but out of loving concern for those committed to their charge.

Self-control means that I say no to all that God forbids and yes to all he ordains; in addition, I am prepared to say no to that which may not be expedient, even though it is not forbidden, and yes to what is not directly ordered, if it would be a blessing.

It is not surprising that Paul found it necessary to teach self-control to the new believers in the churches scattered throughout the Middle East. Many of the converts had come from the ditch of pagan licentiousness, where they had habitually indulged in every conceivable kind of excess. But others had been dug out of legalistic systems where the rules and regulations of man's attempts at self-produced righteousness had harvested a crop of pride and snobbery of the worst kind. They all needed to understand the place of self-control in the life of the believer. What is surprising, however, is that Paul used the subject of self-control in his evangelism.

Self-Control in the Message of the Gospel

Paul's conversations with Felix, the Roman governor in Caesarea, illustrate this beautifully. Paul talked to Felix "about faith in Christ Jesus," but his subject matter was "righteousness, self-control and the judgment to come" (Acts 24:24-25). Felix was described by Tacitus the historian in less than flattering terms. He wrote, "With savagery and lust he exercised the powers of a king with the disposition of a slave." Drusilla, his wife (or more correctly, his third wife), was still under twenty years of age but had already been married and divorced by the ripe old age of sixteen. Clearly Felix could use some insights on self-control. But it is important to note that Paul saw it as a necessary part of the presentation of the gospel of Christ.

Starting with righteousness, the apostle presumably explained that the righteous God has set standards of behavior that are right and which are called righteousness. To live rightly, decisions have to be made about choices that are clearly right or wrong. In Felix's case, they were choices relating to the treatment of women, the exercise of power, and the abuse of privilege. This required self-control because quite often the wrong choices are the most attractive, while the least desirable and the most demanding are the right way to go.

In Felix's case, wrong choices, stemming from a lamentable lack of self-control, had led to all kinds of problems. But Paul was not so much concerned about the immediate problems as the status of Felix in "the judgment to come." For then Felix would have to explain his sinful life and his lack of self-control to the righteous God. At this point Paul no doubt showed how "faith in Christ Jesus" alone could provide the reconciliation and forgiveness his sin had made necessary.

Felix, to the best of our knowledge, though scared at such talk, did not make any public confession of Christ; in fact, when he departed from his post, he left Paul in prison, suggesting that he lost interest not only in the apostle, but also in his message. Perhaps Felix was interested in a gospel that didn't include self-control. If such was the case, he was by no means alone!

We have no way of knowing if Felix understood this message, but we do suspect that many religious leaders of Christ's day did not. He criticized them not so much for their lack of self-control, but for the ways their ideas of self-control left no room for the necessity of salvation through grace. The legalistic system they were used to required all kinds of external discipline. They fasted and prayed and gave alms. They carefully measured the distance they walked on the Sabbath; they were scrupulous about the ceremonial cleansing of vessels and the standards of propriety of dress. But surprisingly the Lord said, "Inside they are full of greed and self-indulgence [lack of self-control]." He painted a gruesome picture as he described them as "whitewashed tombs, which looked beautiful on the outside but on the inside are full of dead men's bones and everything unclean" (Matt. 23:25, 27).

Felix lived a life that openly lacked self-control; the Pharisees lived lives of exacting discipline and control in the externals, but on the inside they were far from controlling the sinful urges and tensions from which overt sinfulness springs. Felix and the Pharisee had in common the need to admit their sinfulness flowing from their self-indulgence, for only then could they find the freshness of forgiveness and the liberty of those set free to serve God.

Self-Control in the Life of the Believer

When the place of self-control in the message of the gospel is understood, there should be no difficulty understanding the ongoing necessity for self-control in the lives of those who find salvation in Christ. For if self-indulgence and lack of self-control result in sin before conversion, they will go on producing sin after conversion. Before conversion these things lead to condemnation, but afterwards there is no condemnation, rather an inconsistency of life and testimony that will make life "ineffective and unproductive" (2 Pet. 1:8). Peter outlined in a most methodical way where self-control fits into the life of the forgiven sinner. He wrote:

> Make every effort to add to your faith goodness; and to goodness, knowledge; and to knowledge, self-control; and to self-control, perseverance; and to perseverance, godliness; and to godliness, brotherly kindness; and to brotherly kindness, love.
>
> *2 Peter 1:5-7*

Peter explained that Christians should do this because they were expected to "participate in the divine nature and escape the corruption in the world caused by evil desires" (2 Pet. 1:4).

There is no such thing as automatic spiritual growth or painless escape from corruption. They come about through careful attention to a succession of understandings and attitudes that lead eventually and inevitably to self-control. If I want to enjoy the power of God in my life, I must control the attitudes and reactions springing from my own sinful heart, which quite clearly hinder the working of the Spirit, who makes that divine nature real. I cannot have the new nature and the old nature living in tandem. It's one or the other. In the same way, if I am serious about escaping the corruption in the world, I must get on the stick as far as self-control is concerned. God is not going to wave in my direction a magic wand that will banish the demons I have been happily entertaining. Neither will he send his celestial cavalry to rescue me at the last minute from the marauding bands of enemies I have been secretly cultivating. I have to say "Be gone" to the demons and "Get lost" to the marauders if I am serious about growth in grace.

The Acts of the Sinful Nature

But we have been dealing in broad generalities, which, while necessary, are not always helpful, as we clearly recognize from the detailed instructions given by the Scriptures on this subject. Paul, immediately prior to listing the fruit of the Spirit in all its beauty, outlined in considerable, sordid detail the obvious acts of the sinful nature:

> Sexual immorality, impurity and debauchery; idolatry and witchcraft; hatred, discord, jealousy, fits of rage, selfish ambition, dissensions, factions and envy; drunkenness, orgies, and the like.
> *Galatians 5:19-21*

There is so much detail in this list of activities attributable to the sinful nature that it is not possible for us to look deeply into it in this book. However, it should be remembered that Paul was speaking about specific issues the churches in Galatia and elsewhere needed to confront if they were to live in the Spirit.

The abuse of sexuality was prevalent and had taken on particularly dangerous overtones because of its link with organized religion. Ancient cultures, so dependent on good crops, had incorporated prostitution into worship experience, believing that it would honor the gods of the fertility cult and guarantee the produce required. No doubt they also enjoyed the unrestrained, uninhibited sexual excess! Paul needed to remind the believers living in that kind of environment of a higher, nobler view of both sexuality and productivity, because both were related to the Creator God and not the gods of human manufacture.

"Impurity and debauchery" followed hard on the heels of sexual immorality. They related to the human drive for unrestrained living, whatever its consequences. Everything became permissible in such an environment, because those who participated in such things also participated in an idolatry that gave total license. Idols were no threat to unrestrained living because they had been made in man's image and the gods they represented were notorious in the realm of legend and fable for their unrestrained, uninhibited life-style. The gods of the Greeks simply magnified the excesses of their adherents.

Witchcraft was also involved. When we realize that the Greek word for witchcraft is the word from which we get pharmacist, we have no difficulty understanding the place of drugs in this kind of approach to life. In fact, in the light of what has been said, one would almost expect drugs to figure somewhere. Paul, in his dealings with pagan society, recognized the connection between the life-style of the people and their philosophy of life, and he endeavored to show the new believers how they needed to call that pagan life-style by its true name and to take steps to put some distance between themselves and it. That major change required self-control.

Turning to interpersonal relationships, the apostle showed how incorrect behavior produces all manner of aberrations in this vital, important area of human experience. Citing such traits as "hatred, discord, jealousy, fits of rage, selfish ambition, dissensions, factions"—all of which are most familiar to all of us—Paul roundly condemned them as "acts of the sinful nature."

We may be inclined to be more tolerant and explain our actions in terms of unfortunate heredity—"My mother was Irish, you know"—or psychological insight—"My father abused us as children, you see." While there is no denying the place of heredity and genetics, environment and situations in the forming of personality, it must be stressed that they can only produce a proclivity toward action and that the *will* still determines whether the proclivity be rejected or followed. It is not good enough to excuse behavior by blaming it on a mother long gone or an environment that disappeared under the real-estate developer's bulldozer years ago. Behavior ultimately is the result of choice, whatever factors figured in the making of the choice. Proper choices require self-control, and that means self-control in things like anger, jealousy, selfish ambition, and the like.

Not for Self-Improvement

It would be wrong of us to assume all the Greeks of Paul's day were committed to unrestrained living of the kind described above. In marked contrast to the free wheelers, there were considerable numbers who were rigid disciplinarians. The Stoics, for instance, were committed to a life of phenomenal control, but it was far different from Paul's Christian approach to self-mastery.

The Stoic worshiped at the shrine of sovereign self-will. If he was confronted by things he could handle through discipline and application, he did it. When circumstances that were too much for him came his way, he prided himself in steeling his nerve to accept the unacceptable and to tolerate the inevitable, so even from "defeat" he could snatch "victory" for indomitable self-will. This led to a kind of fatalistic, yet arrogant approach to life. Stoics detested meekness;

humility to them was a bore. They were the ancient parallels to the modern "grit your teeth and make things happen" people.

Paul was not talking about self-will that was sovereign, even though his position was much closer to these people's than the others. His doctrine of self-control stemmed from the truth of the Spirit's presence in the life of the believer, to give courage and determination where previously they did not exist. Far from encouraging a colossal determination for self-improvement in terms of self-effort, Paul called for a monumental dependence upon and obedience to the indwelling Spirit, which would be glorifying to God through self-control rather than putting another proud man atop the monument to self-effort and self-improvement.

Furthermore, when Paul spoke of self-control, he had in mind not so much the personal improvement of the believer as the well-being of those among whom he lived, the success of the ministry in which the believer was involved, and above all else the glory of God. Self-control, rather than being an effort to make things better for the Christian, was an expression of appreciation for the miracle of redeeming grace and the unlimited forgiveness for deeds that were sinful because of lack of self-control.

Neither was Paul's self-control designed to catch the eye of God, with a view to special reward for sacrificial services rendered. It was rather a warmhearted demonstration of gratitude for salvation offered at no cost to the recipient, but at awful cost to the donor.

In a sense, quite a lot of contemporary self-control, even among believers, has self-improvement as its goal. Dieting has reached faddish proportions, and often the motivation for it has more to do with Jane Fonda and the "in" lean look than with a conviction about good, God's gifts, and healthy bodies as the vehicles of divine activity. Exercise seems to be designed in many people's eyes to prolong life, which in the case of a believer would presumably postpone heaven! An irony indeed, when we remember the gusto with which hymns of anticipated glory are sung! But if fitness is seen as a means of clearer thinking and greater stamina and swifter resilience, so that more energy can be devoted to the cause of Christ and the well-being of society, then self-control will be God honoring rather than just self-improving.

This comes through most clearly in Paul's autobiographical passage on self-control:

Do you not know that in a race all the runners run, but only one gets the prize? Run in such a way as to get the prize. Everyone who competes in the games goes into strict training. They do it to get a crown that will not last; but we do it to get a crown that will last forever. Therefore I do not run like a man running aimlessly; I do not fight like a man beating the air. No, I beat my body and make it my slave so that after I have preached to others I myself will not be disqualified for the prize.
1 Corinthians 9:24-27

Taking the analogy of the athlete, which was most familiar to Corinthians, who attended the famous Isthmian Games held in the environs of their city, Paul talked to them about self-mastery with a Christian objective. His first concern in using the athletic analogy was to get believers to take their Christianity as seriously as the committed athlete takes his sport. Anyone who knows anything about the successful athlete knows that his performance on the day of the event is the culmination of a great many hours' training, many disciplines and sacrifices, and innumerable hard decisions. This kind of mindset about Christian life and ministry is what Paul was looking for in those for whom he had accepted spiritual oversight. The Christian who shows up at the church minutes before the service, unprepared and ill equipped for worship is as out of line as the team player who arrives at the stadium minutes before the start of the game, lacking equipment, concentration, and conditioning! The preacher who ad-libs his way through a teaching engagement with considerable evidence that he has not done his homework is like the athlete who reports to training camp fifty pounds overweight. He just isn't on track!

Second, the Christian, like the athlete, needs to know what his goals are. When I talked to Robin Yount, the shortstop of the Milwaukee Brewers, a couple of days before the start of the 1982 World Series, he gave every indication of knowing what he wanted to achieve. He was uninterested in the adoring chants of the fans demanding he be Most Valuable Player in the American League. His goal was to win the World Series. As far as he was concerned, it didn't matter if it took four games or seven. They were aiming at being world champions, and they had determined to give it their best effort. If it was good enough, fine; if not, they would improve and go for it in 1983! Robin and his teammates knew what they were after.

Critics of the modern athletic scene might respond, "What a shame that grown men should put so much effort into getting a Series ring and a few thousand more bucks." These sentiments may be partially valid, as Paul showed when he spoke of the goal of the athletes of his day being able to wear a wreath of laurels that would quickly wither. But there was no doubt about Paul's conviction that Christians need goals similar to those of the athlete, and they are not to be petty, unchallenging goals either!

"We do it," Paul wrote, "to get a crown that will last forever." The goals of the Christian, which are a factor in his life of disciplined self-mastery, are eternity and eternal values. Those things that matter on earth are not unimportant, but those things that count in glory are all-important. To Paul, aiming high meant living life in the light of eternity and gearing activities and commitments to things of eternal significance.

Paul is also careful to show that eternal goals are achieved as intermediate objectives are being achieved. Robin arrived at the World Series first of all by playing 162 games in order to win the American League Eastern Division. That won, the team turned their attention to the five-game series for the American League Championship, and only when that was won could they then tackle the World Series.

The Christian doesn't operate on the basis of hitting eternal goals and wearing unfading crowns in the here and now; he has to win many a divisional contest before he can start getting excited about such things. That involves "strict training," dedicated application to competing "in such a way as to get the prize," and careful attention to details that will ensure that he "will not be disqualified for the prize."

Paul was never worried about using mixed metaphors and was not at all loath to go in one easy movement from the running track to the boxing ring, if it would serve his purpose. His Christian life was like a road race where the end had to be kept in sight, but it was also a fight with a spiritual opponent of great strength and ability. And it was also a fight against his own nature. Many a boxer has lost the fight on the scales before ever reaching the ring, and Paul had no intention of getting into the fray of the Christian life with a glass jaw or a potbelly.

Self-control looks at the opposition outside and takes stock of the opponent inside. It measures the strength of the forces to be beaten in conflict and the costly means required to do it, but also identifies the weak spots on the inside and carefully measures the steps necessary to obviate them. "Know yourself" is good advice if it includes knowing your weaknesses. Then be tough on them, like the boxer who knows his midriff is slack and then works out on the medicine ball for hour after painful hour until the muscles are like a washboard. Many Christian lives have shipwrecked precisely because they did not take careful stock of weaknesses and take meticulous steps to deal with them. Some men in privileged positions of ministry have enjoyed the attention of women helped by the ministry. But instead of reading the danger signals of their own obvious delight in such attention, they have basked in it till they have been seduced by it. Saying no in a squeaky voice is no way to handle seduction designed to discredit a ministry or disqualify a Christian's testimony. Seeing the seduction a mile off and putting another mile's distance between yourself and it is the way to go.

The Example of Gethsemane

Whenever the struggle for self-control gets hard—and for those who take it seriously it always will—there is no better exercise than to look again at Gethsemane. See there the anguished struggle of the Son of Man contemplating being made sin, being separated from the Father, bearing the law's awful curse, and tasting death for every man. Hear again the words, "If it is possible, may this cup be taken from me" (Matt. 26:39) and feel the tension. But then read the words of the ultimate self-controlled life, "Not my will, but yours be done" (Luke 22:42). This is not the self-discipline of a man on a diet for his figure or jogging for his health. The Son of Man brought mind, body, and soul into subjection to the will of God for the well-being of a lost humanity.

When the struggle against sin or the heavy demands of disciplined living for the sake of others gets a little too heavy, turn again to the Lord who was dead and is alive. Thank him for Gethsemane. And in your own heart, aided by his Spirit, breathe those words, "Not my will, but yours be done." Claim God's power to make the necessary decisions and adjustments to make it stick. That is self-control; that is Spirit life.

QUESTIONS

1. How does self-control free the Christian? What are the two ditches beside the highway of freedom described by the author? How will these be influenced by self-control?

2. Why did Paul preach self-control to Felix? How did Felix respond? Why did Jesus criticize the Pharisees' attitude toward self-control? How did they respond? What did these two have in common? How did the first-century Greeks parallel Felix and the Pharisees in their attitudes toward self-control?

3. What is the role of self-control in the Christian life? What did Paul envision as its most important influence?

4. What should be the ultimate goal of self-control?

11
No Orchids for Wisconsin

Orchids grow wild in the steamy humidity of equatorial regions, but they don't do well in Wisconsin. Palm trees flourish in the mild breezes of the tropics, but they shrivel and die in Wisconsin. It's a matter of climate, of course, and when it comes to Wisconsin winters, we just don't talk about climate. We bundle up and go skiing!

Climate is the key to spiritual growth, too. Paul wrote: "Those who belong to Christ Jesus have crucified the sinful nature with its passions and desires. Since we live by the Spirit, let us keep in step with the Spirit" (Gal. 5:24-25).

In the same way that temperature, humidity, and rainfall determine climate and growth, so "belonging to Christ," "crucifying the sinful nature," and "living by the Spirit" create the climate in which Spirit life flourishes.

Christians know, in theory, that they belong to Christ, but they struggle with the implications. Simply put, I can't belong to two opposing parties at the same time, and unfortunately my selfish interests are often in opposition to the interests and claims of Christ. The tension of submitting myself to Christ when it means surrendering such personal "rights" as privacy, the use of time, and expenditure of money can be quite severe. Many Christian lives have become shriveled and dead at this point. But the challenge must be faced because Christ's claims to his disciples' lives are based on the fact that the Father gave us to him (John 17:6). Furthermore the redemption that Christ accomplished on the cross means, as Paul explained it, "You are not your own; you were bought at a price" (1 Cor. 6:19-20).

There was a time in my youthful Christian experience when I perceived the claims of Christ on my life to be unreasonable. It was only when I confronted the fact that my life had been bought by Christ and I had been presented by my Creator to Christ that I realized it was I who was being unreasonable, not Christ. God was laying claim to what was his, not mine. I was holding on to what was no longer mine, but his. There and then I submitted myself gladly to "belonging to Christ," to being what he wanted me to be.

"Crucifying the sinful nature" is not quite so easy to understand, and it is certainly not easy to implement. That we have a bias to sin is all too apparent to all of us, so we don't need to identify the reality of a sinful nature. That this sinful nature is the source of sin is equally clear. But what is not always clear is the fact that Christ's death would have been inadequate if it had dealt only with sins and done nothing about the sinful nature. Doctors do not treat symptoms and ignore causes. They try to treat both.

That Christ died for our sins is a fundamental and glorious belief of Christians, but what about the sinful nature that produced the sins? Did Christ's death do anything about that? On this point Christians have long differed and sometimes loudly argued. Some have argued that the sinful nature, having been crucified, must be dead; and, therefore, if they believe that to be a fact, they will be free from it, because it has been eradicated. The problem with this approach is that even those who propound the theory clearly struggle with it in practice.

In my opinion, Scripture teaches that when I come to the cross for forgiveness of sins, I also want to be done with the sinful nature that produced the sins. I wish to be changed from the person who was previously dominated by the power of sin in my life. Therefore, as I kneel at the cross for forgiveness I also leave at the cross my previous approach to life. I ask to be forgiven for stealing, but I also leave a covetous attitude at the cross. The boisterous days of cussing, hard drinking, and wife beating are forgiven and forgotten, but the anger and brutishness that caused them are also repented of and left at the cross. I ask Christ to stamp them with the mark of his cross. They receive from him the kiss of death. This does not eradicate them; neither does it mean I cannot resurrect them. But it does mean a decision about them has been made in the light of the cross, and the rest of my days will be spent dying to the things for which I previously lived.

"Living in the Spirit" is the positive side of the coin. When God created the heavens and the earth, the Spirit was moving, and he has been on the move ever since. It was the Spirit who inspired the prophets and apostles. We must thank him for the Scriptures, which make us wise. He was the means whereby Christ was born; we honor him for making the Incarnation possible. He strangely moved on our cold hearts to warm us to Christ; in some indefinable way he opened our blind eyes to truth without in any way abusing our God-given gift of free will. And it was through him that Christ was born in our hearts.

It is easy to see, therefore, that we do live in the Spirit, because without his ministry, we would still be "dead in trespasses and sins."

But Paul means more than this. He wants believers to grasp the astounding fact that the Spirit himself is our indwelling resource of life. Without his power, theology would be another philosophy, theory without practice, truth without reality. But through his power, ever available to us, we have the means of putting into gear all that the Word of God puts in our heads. To believe this is to believe in the immensity of spiritual potential and the inevitability of spiritual blessing.

To grow the Spirit life, we need the right climate. To want Spirit life under any other conditions is to want the impossible. To expect Spirit life to flourish in other conditions is to live exiled in fantasy land. Why? For the same reason that wanting orchids to grow in Wisconsin and expecting them to flourish in subarctic conditions doesn't make it happen. Orchids don't grow in Wisconsin, but they sure do flourish in Singapore!